Jesus *the* God-Man

Jesus *the* God-Man

THE UNITY AND DIVERSITY OF THE GOSPEL PORTRAYALS

Darrell L. Bock
with Benjamin I. Simpson

BakerAcademic
a division of Baker Publishing Group
Grand Rapids, Michigan

Published by Baker Academic
a division of Baker Publishing Group
P.O. Box 6287, Grand Rapids, MI 49516-6287
www.bakeracademic.com

Printed in the United States of America

Library of Congress Cataloging-in-Publication Data
Names: Bock, Darrell L., author.
Title: Jesus the God-man : the unity and diversity of the gospel portrayals / Darrell L. Bock, with Benjamin I. Simpson.
Description: Grand Rapids : Baker Academic, 2016. | Includes bibliographical references and index.
Identifiers: LCCN 2015048414 | ISBN 9780801097782 (pbk.)
Subjects: LCSH: Jesus Christ—Biography—History and criticism. | Bible. Gospels—Criticism, interpretation, etc.
Classification: LCC BT301.9 .B63 2016 | DDC 232—dc23
LC record available at http://lccn.loc.gov/2015048414

16 17 18 19 20 21 22 7 6 5 4 3 2 1

In keeping with biblical principles of creation stewardship, Baker Publishing Group advocates the responsible use of our natural resources. As a member of the Green Press Initiative, our company uses recycled paper when possible. The text paper of this book is composed in part of post-consumer waste.

With appreciation to Sally Bock and Amber Simpson,
for partnership, support, and being there as gifts from God

Contents

Preface

I have long wanted to write this book. It has an interesting prehistory that also helps to explain its origins and importance. In the first edition of *Jesus according to Scripture*,[1] the discussion of Jesus's teaching as a whole made up the final section, part 4. I had hoped that it would be seen as a useful synthesis of what the Gospels are doing. As can sometimes happen in a long and complex book, the part the author most wanted to be seen as the climactic section was lost in all the detail that preceded it. So I have decided to expand and develop this section and let it stand on its own, updating and reworking the material in the process.

Part of what I wanted to show and now can make even more clear is how the Synoptics and John work on their own and in relationship to each other. In the interim, I have thought a lot more about some of the ideas I first expressed in the concluding section of that book. My key premise is that the Synoptics primarily present Jesus through what he does. They reveal who Jesus is from the earth up by taking readers from categories we normally apply to people and then showing how it dawned on his followers that Jesus uniquely transcends those categories. John goes the other direction. We know from John

1. Darrell L. Bock, *Jesus according to Scripture: Restoring the Portrait from the Gospels* (Grand Rapids: Baker Academic, 2002; 2nd ed., forthcoming).

1:1 that Jesus is divine and took on flesh. John declares who Jesus is from the start. This difference has led believers to rely heavily on John. In the process, the Synoptics have been less appreciated for how they present Jesus, since John does much heavy lifting for us.

What makes this difference important is that all of us must approach Jesus from the earth up. None of us comes with an inherent understanding of all that he is. Someone must explain Jesus and his uniqueness to us. This book aims to retell that story and show how the Gospels do it. The hope is that in doing so, a fresh appreciation for how to read the Gospels and understand how Scripture presents Jesus will emerge for you as it has for me. My desire is that this book will not only prove to be a useful summary of key elements in the Gospels' portrait of Jesus but also serve to open up fresh avenues for understanding how the Gospels work within the canon.

So what was originally intended as a climactic section in a developing inductive study of Jesus in the Gospels we now present as a stand-alone synthetic look at Jesus from the core documents of the early church. By highlighting the inherent unity and consistency among the Gospels, I hope to instill a greater appreciation for how to read the Gospels and how to talk about Jesus to those who are curious to understand what his life and ministry sought to achieve.

We continue to be grateful to Dallas Theological Seminary for its support. Mark Bailey and Mark Yarbrough deserve thanks for their encouragement of our writing. Joseph Fantin, Mike Burer, Will Johnston, Samuel Chia, Terri Moore, and James Davis need to be added to the names of supportive New Testament colleagues. Thanks also goes to the staff at the Hendricks Center, including Bill Hendricks, Pam Cole, Kymberli Cook, and Mikel DelRosario. Heather Zimmerman at the Center worked on a related project that also fed into this work.

Of course we also thank our wives, Sally Bock and Amber Simpson, who put up with much when we undertook this project.

Darrell L. Bock
Ben Simpson
October 15, 2015

Abbreviations

General and Bibliographic

//	paralleled by (*see also* par.)
ABRL	Anchor Bible Reference Library
AD	anno Domini
ASV	American Standard Version
AT	author's translation
BC	before Christ
BECNT	Baker Exegetical Commentary on the New Testament
ca.	circa, approximately
CEB	Common English Bible
cf.	*confer*, compare
chap.	chapter
DJG[1]	*Dictionary of Jesus and the Gospels*. Edited by Joel B. Green and Scot McKnight. First ed. Downers Grove, IL: InterVarsity, 1992.
e.g.	*exempli gratia*, for example
esp.	especially
frg.	fragment
i.e.	*id est*, that is
JSHJ	*Journal for the Study of the Historical Jesus*
JSNT	*Journal for the Study of the New Testament*
JSNTSup	Journal for the Study of the New Testament Supplement Series
KJV	King James Version
L	material unique to Luke
M	material unique to Matthew
n.	note
NASB	New American Standard Bible

NIV	New International Version (2011)
NIV 1984	New International Version (1984)
NKJV	New King James Version
NRSV	New Revised Standard Version
NT	New Testament
OT	Old Testament
par.	and its parallel(s)
Q	material common to Matthew and Luke
RSV	Revised Standard Version
SNTSU	Studien zum Neuen Testament und seiner Umwelt
WUNT	Wissenschaftliche Untersuchungen zum Neuen Testament
×	number of times a term appears

Old Testament

Gen.	Genesis
Exod.	Exodus
Lev.	Leviticus
Num.	Numbers
Deut.	Deuteronomy
Josh.	Joshua
Judg.	Judges
Ruth	Ruth
1–2 Sam.	1–2 Samuel
1–2 Kings	1–2 Kings
1–2 Chron.	1–2 Chronicles
Ezra	Ezra
Neh.	Nehemiah
Esther	Esther
Job	Job
Ps(s).	Psalm(s)
Prov.	Proverbs
Eccles.	Ecclesiastes
Song	Song of Songs
Isa.	Isaiah
Jer.	Jeremiah
Lam.	Lamentations
Ezek.	Ezekiel
Dan.	Daniel
Hosea	Hosea
Joel	Joel
Amos	Amos
Obad.	Obadiah
Jon.	Jonah
Mic.	Micah
Nah.	Nahum
Hab.	Habakkuk
Zeph.	Zephaniah
Hag.	Haggai
Zech.	Zechariah
Mal.	Malachi

New Testament

Matt.	Matthew
Mark	Mark
Luke	Luke
John	John
Acts	Acts
Rom.	Romans

1–2 Cor.	1–2 Corinthians
Gal.	Galatians
Eph.	Ephesians
Phil.	Philippians
Col.	Colossians
1–2 Thess.	1–2 Thessalonians
1–2 Tim.	1–2 Timothy
Titus	Titus
Philem.	Philemon
Heb.	Hebrews
James	James
1–2 Pet.	1–2 Peter
1–3 John	1–3 John
Jude	Jude
Rev.	Revelation

Old Testament Apocrypha

2 Esd.	2 Esdras
1–4 Macc.	1–4 Maccabees
Sir.	Sirach
Tob.	Tobit
Wis.	Wisdom of Solomon

Other Ancient Sources

Ant.	Josephus, *Jewish Antiquities*
As. Mos.	*Assumption of Moses*
b.	Babylonian Talmud
2 Bar.	*2 Baruch*
CD	Cairo Genizah copy of the *Damascus Document*
Dial.	Justin Martyr, *Dialogue with Trypho*
1 En.	*1 Enoch*
Jub.	*Jubilees*
m.	Mishnah
Ned.	tractate *Nedarim*
Pss. Sol.	*Psalms of Solomon*
1QM	*Milḥamah = War Scroll*, from Qumran Cave 1
1QS	*Serek Hayaḥad = Rule of the Community*, from Qumran Cave 1
4Q174	*Florilegium*, also *Midrash on Eschatology*, copy a, from Qumran Cave 4
4QpIsa[d]	*Isaiah Pesher*, copy d = 4Q164, from Qumran Cave 4
4QPrNab	*Prayer of Nabonidus* (Aramaic) = 4Q242, from Qumran Cave 4
11QT[a]	*Temple Scroll*, copy a = 11Q19, from Qumran Cave 11
Šabb.	tractate *Šabbat*
Sanh.	tractate *Sanhedrin*
Sib. Or.	*Sibylline Oracles*
Spec. Laws	Philo, *Special Laws*
T. Benj.	*Testament of Benjamin*
T. Dan	*Testament of Dan*
T. Iss.	*Testament of Issachar*
T. Jud.	*Testament of Judah*

Introduction

> And the prophetic dignity in Christ leads us to know that in the sum of doctrine as he has given it to us all parts of perfect wisdom are contained.[1]
>
> Calvin, *Institutes of the Christian Religion* 2.15.2

Jesus has always been a topic of intense conversation and controversy. A sense has always existed that he was a unique individual and that in him much wisdom is to be found. Yet controversy also has always surrounded him. Is he a prophet, the Messiah, or something profoundly more? Or was he crucified because his claims or those of his followers far outstripped his person? This is part of the story the Gospels tell and try to answer by showing the unique character of his life, both in terms of his actions and the titles applied to him.

The study of Jesus has always had to interact with an attempt to explain the seemingly curious result of his life, a crucifixion grounded in rejection, and the emergence of a religion rooted in worshipful reception that eventually spanned the globe. Its beginning in a small, fringe part of the Roman Empire belies the scope of what eventually

1. John Calvin, *Institutes of the Christian Religion*, ed. J. T. McNeill, trans. F. L. Battles, 2 vols. (Philadelphia: Westminster, 1960), 1:496.

emerged from the life of this man from Galilee. This book is about the study of that contrast, its causes and results. That contrast is what makes studying Jesus and understanding the Gospels so fascinating.

Recently three developments have impacted the study of Jesus in the Gospels. First, there has been a shift of focus from debates about the historical Jesus, which are still discussed in NT studies, to concern for "Jesus remembered," or how his impact is seen in the narrative theology of the Gospels.[2] It is an important development because now the "quest" is not so much for the Jesus behind the Gospels or for a reconstructed Jesus, but for the Jesus of the documents that ended up being the portrait that produced historic impact on the world.

Second, alongside this has come a shift from focusing the discussion of Jesus from his sayings and titles to his actions. The roots of this shift go back to the early days of the third quest for the historical Jesus, and the new focus has led to a greater appreciation for how the events in Jesus's life point to who he portrayed himself to be.[3] This book will work with these shifts, since they are important in understanding Jesus and his ministry.

Third, there is a greater appreciation for the role of narrative in presenting theology. This fits with the emphasis on actions and deeds. It also parallels how the texts show Jesus handling the issue of his activity and person. When John the Baptist sent emissaries to ask Jesus if he was the one to come or whether they should expect another, Jesus replied with a listing of his actions that told a narrative about the arrival of the new age (Luke 7:18–23//Matt. 11:2–6). This study of Jesus will keep all three of these recent developments in mind, since they have the potential to open up fresh ways to appreciate what the evangelists saw Jesus doing and saying. (The order of doing and saying is important here.)

One other idea is crucial to this book. It is the proposition that three Gospels tell the story of Jesus mostly from the earth up, while

2. J. D. G. Dunn, *Jesus Remembered* (Grand Rapids: Eerdmans, 2003).

3. The core feature of the Third Quest is to root Jesus's ministry in its Second Temple Jewish background, something that will be prominent in the present book. Among major proponents in recent times, covering a range of approaches, are Martin Hengel, Ben Meyer, George Caird, E. P. Sanders, John Meier, J. D. G. Dunn, Tom Wright, I. Howard Marshall, Craig Evans, Ben Witherington, Scot McKnight, Robert Webb, and Craig Keener.

John tells the story from heaven down. The difference is important. The path the Synoptics set has been largely lost on the church today, which prefers that John do the heavy lifting in presenting Jesus. Jesus's uniqueness is something we can more deeply appreciate when we look at him from the earth up.[4]

The church's presentation of Jesus includes the claim that here is a human being unlike any other. He is God incarnate. So how does one come to see and appreciate this claim about who Jesus is and what he is about? How does someone grow in their understanding of who Jesus is if they start with him as being simply a great human being? In Matthew, Mark, and Luke, each Gospel in its own way makes its case and points to how monotheistically oriented Jews came to affirm a uniquely exalted status for Jesus among all who have trod the earth. The church needs to relearn this way of presenting Jesus. Much of this volume is an effort to explain how this can be done. So we offer this account of how Scripture presents Jesus, mostly from the earth up, and how he delivered his message about kingdom hope. Along the way, energized by this extraordinary figure, we discover how that kingdom's activity fulfills promises God had made long ago.

Christ's teaching and the works of apostolic reflection about God's work through him in the NT have served as a hub for instruction that has guided the church and influenced culture over the centuries. A crucial portion of that valuable deposit of divine truth is the evangelists' portrayal of Jesus's teaching. So we consider the major themes and actions of Jesus's ministry as the Gospel writers present them. Under each key theme, we try to single out whether the emphasis is the concern of any particular evangelist or is a shared concern. We also point out any particular emphases of any evangelist within each topic. Finally, we pay special attention to how "public" or "private" the teaching in question was as the evangelists portray it. Here we

4. A careful study going in a similar direction on how the Gospels handle the Hebrew Scriptures and Christology in the presentation of Jesus is by Richard B. Hays, *Reading Backwards: Figural Christology and the Fourfold Gospel Witness* (Waco: Baylor University Press, 2014). What he calls "figural," we call "pattern prophecy." He argues that when one reads narratively, it is important to read both forward and retrospectively to appreciate all that a Gospel is doing. His chapter on Mark is especially clear in presenting this kind of reading. What he has done for the use of the OT we are applying to the reading of the Synoptics as a whole.

find a clue as to what Jesus said to all versus what he taught just to the disciples.

The synthesis does not proceed Gospel by Gospel, but thematically. We consider what Jesus presented as teaching or reflect on the significance of his actions. The evangelists' narrative commentary is excluded from consideration. Elsewhere I have developed that other approach to reading by working through the pericope units of the Gospels in *Jesus according to Scripture*.[5] Now I do something different. I gather together the key strands of that story, strands said to go back to Jesus. What the evangelists passed on has come to us through tradition and from the choices that the given evangelists made concerning what they wished to show about Jesus. The church regards what is passed on to be the result of the active work of God's Spirit leading the authors to write what they do. Such teaching no doubt was passed on with the conviction that it was of value to the original audiences of each Gospel. Those churches passed these testimonies on to later generations. They believed that these accounts reflect what Jesus was about in preaching the kingdom and in doing the work God had sent him to do. Thus the teaching of the Gospels is pastoral at its core. It seeks to ground readers solidly in a walk with God through the development of a devotion to God, appreciating what God has done through Jesus. The church, in turn, recognizing the value of what was recorded for nurture in the faith, embraced these works and their portraits of Jesus as faithful expressions of what it means to confess Jesus and follow him. There can be no better capstone to a personal study of Jesus than to focus on the key themes of his life and ministry and their connection to his own teaching and actions.

5. Darrell L. Bock, *Jesus according to Scripture: Restoring the Portrait from the Gospels* (Grand Rapids: Baker Academic, 2002; 2nd ed., forthcoming).

1

Preparation: Birth, John the Baptist, and the Temptations

The Endorsed and Qualified Anointed One

> For one must reckon *a priori* with the possibility—even with the probability—first, that in his teaching and life Jesus accomplished something new from which the first Christians had to proceed in their attempt to explain his person and work; second, that their experience of Christ exhibited special features not present in any obvious analogy to related religious forms. It is simply unscholarly prejudice methodically to exclude from the beginning this possibility—this probability.[1]

Jesus's teaching was unique and made unique claims. But how in the world did the church reach this understanding? More important, how in the world did first-century Jewish disciples grasp it? In the face of a host of gods and idols in their world, what caused those

1. Oscar Cullmann, *The Christology of the New Testament*, rev. ed. (London: SCM, 1959), 5.

who believed in one Creator God to affirm that Jesus's relationship to God was neither polytheism nor a violation of the faith in the one God of the Shema? It is that journey portrayed in the Gospels that the theology of the Jesus of Scripture explores.

That transformation of thinking out of a Second Temple Jewish context is why understanding him and his portrait in the Gospels is so important. Jesus claims to give unique insight into God's plan and to present the way to divine fellowship and blessing. Many of these claims are rooted in the Jewish foundations to which Jesus belonged. However, Jesus's teaching on hope led to an appreciation that he was speaking about more than a plan for Israel. The nation's calling always had been to serve as a means of blessing for the world. Jesus's starting point involved a call to Israel to prepare for the promised completion of what God had started with them. However, that plan, at least as far back as Isa. 40–66, not to mention all the way back to Gen. 12:3, had foreseen the inclusion of the Gentile nations within God's blessing. Jesus's teaching ultimately aims at this comprehensive goal of blessing extended to all the righteous by faith from every nation. God's promise, given long ago, had affirmed that blessing would come for the righteous in the whole world. We turn our attention to the major strands of Jesus's teachings and actions because through their interplay we see what his ministry was all about.[2] So we start with Jesus's birth, John the Baptist, and the temptations.

Incarnation: Jesus the Sent Son/Messiah

This initial chapter focuses on the frame around which Jesus's ministry appears. The incarnation emerges as part of a reflective introduction about Jesus the Word incarnate (John 1:1–18) or as part of the emphasis in the presentation of Jesus's infancy in two of the Synoptics (Matt. 1–2; Luke 1–2). John plays all of his cards from the start, from the very first verse: "In the beginning was the Word, and the Word was with God, and the Word was God." Jesus is affirmed as

2. The survey is mostly thematic rather than chronological, but where sequence matters, we will pay attention to it, as with the framing of Jesus's ministry in birth, baptism, and the temptations.

the Creator (John 1:1–3), a role for God. John tells the story of Jesus very much from heaven down.

The Synoptics take a different route. Mark simply starts with the ministry of John the Baptist and Jesus's acceptance of baptism from him. This frames Jesus's work in the eschatological hope and call to repent that John preached. It means that Jesus affirmed and endorsed John's call to Israel to turn back to God and prepare for God's coming deliverance. In both Matthew and Luke, the emphasis is on how Jesus's birth fulfilled divine promises.

In Matthew, the emphasis is on themes tied to messianic promise or the patterns of Israel's history, including themes about conflict and rejection. As a narrator Matthew points out how Jesus fulfills promises about where the Messiah would be born (Mic. 5:2), how Jesus replicates the calling of Israel as Son (Hosea 11:1), how he mirrors the suffering of the nation (Jer. 31:15), and how "God with us" would be born of a virgin (Isa. 7:14). In Matthew's introduction, the portrait of "God with us" is the dominating note that implies the presence of the divine in Jesus. Jesus is clearly sent as part of a divine program already suggested in Scripture. The virgin birth points to the start of a unique journey for, with, and through Jesus. Yet this is still from the earth up, as those around Jesus's birth are seen as coming to grips with what all of this means.

Luke's infancy account goes in a similar direction but with less explicitness. A virgin birth is described, but Isaiah is not noted. The Scripture is present, but not in narrative notes of citation. Rather, hymns of scripturally rooted praise frame the birth as the arrival of hope. In Matthew, Jesus's birth comes with suffering and rejection from the start, with the slaying of the infants in Bethlehem as Rachel weeps for her children. The notes in Matthew show the conflict from the start. In contrast, Jesus's arrival in Luke is one of continuous joy, with the only hint of trouble coming near the end of the infancy sequence in Simeon's word to Mary and in Jesus's independent act when he stays behind in Jerusalem and declares that he must be about his Father's work (Luke 2:49 NKJV).

In Luke, a series of three hymns presents the core theology. Mary is thankful that she can experience the grace of God as a humble woman of the nation and anticipates a just reversal, where the arrogant are brought down and the humble are exalted (Luke 1:46–55, the Magnificat). Zechariah praises God for raising up a Davidic Horn to rescue God's people: Messiah is pictured as the rising sun of the morning, bringing dawn to darkness (Luke 1:68–79, the Benedictus). Simeon can return to God through death in peace because he has seen God's salvation, with Messiah again seen as a light, a revelation to Gentiles, and a glory for Israel (Luke 2:29–32, Nunc Dimittus). So the note of explicit incarnation is less obvious in Luke. Rather, what dominates is the realization of God's program and the hope it generates. The themes of joy and celebration arise in light of the fulfillment of divine promise. The hymns that reveal the theology of hope invoke the Abrahamic and Davidic covenants (Luke 1:31–35, 68–69) and point to Jesus as son of David, seated on the throne that God promised to David's house. Here "son" takes on an ambiguity early in the account, for the king could be seen as a son (2 Sam. 7:8–18).

The Synoptics take the rest of the narrative to describe the kind of person Jesus is and to give the significance of his coming. Sometimes by looking back, aware of how the story ends, we miss how the story emerged in its unfolding and the struggle that faced those who followed him. We have a hard time understanding their struggle to appreciate what they were seeing at the time. Hindsight is twenty-twenty. So we can miss how the account builds up gradually to display who Jesus is for the evangelists. Knowing the end of the mystery, we forget the drama that takes us up many steps, one step at a time, to its disclosure. The birth of Jesus frames his ministry as one sent from God, the bearer of a special message as a result of a special birth. Just how special all of this was and what it all meant requires the rest of the story. The risk is that in arriving at the finish line of an exalted confession, we forget how we arrive there and how others got there as well. Luke's infancy account ends with Jesus presenting his sense of vocation to his parents. He must be about the work of his Father. That brings us to the preparatory work of John the Baptist.

Jesus's Submitting to John's Baptism and the Divine Voice

Jesus's choice to share in John's baptism means that he was identifying with John's call to the nation of Israel to repent and prepare for the coming of God's kingdom. The point is important because some argue that Jesus taught wisdom and ethics and avoided talk about judgment or things that reflected Jewish apocalyptic hope, expecting a divine vindication for the righteous. John clearly fits in this latter category of teaching, so Jesus's submitting to baptism by John indicates an acceptance of that message. Thus it is a flawed reading of Jesus to force a choice between a Jesus who called for ethical or moral integrity before God and one who preached about the coming judgment and vindication of God. As we shall see, Jesus taught and reflected on both ideas.

John's ministry is corroborated by Josephus (*Ant.* 18.5.2 §§116–19),[3] who points out that many Jews saw the defeat of Herod's army by the Nabatean ruler Aretas IV as divine punishment for Herod's slaying of John. Josephus reports that John urged people to receive baptism as well as to cultivate virtue and practice piety and justice. Josephus portrays this baptism as an act of purification. Virtue, piety, and justice are concepts that Josephus's Roman audience could grasp. Herod slew John the Baptist because he feared John's persuasive power with the people.

The eschatological elements of John's ministry, drawing from Isa. 40:3, also have parallels in Judaism. The Qumran community appealed to this text for their separatism and desire to await the approach of God's redemption (1QS 8.14; 9.19–20). The Qumranians applied this text to justify withdrawing from corrupt society and religious practices in order to study the law in holy preparation for God's coming.

All the Gospels connect John to this Isa. 40 tradition when introducing his ministry.[4] John's baptism makes a call for righteousness

3. For a thorough discussion of this text, see John Meier, *A Marginal Jew: Rethinking the Historical Jesus,* 2 vols., ABRL (New York: Doubleday, 1994), 2:56–62. In this discussion Meier states that Josephus had no desire to report the more eschatological features of John's message, such as judgment. For apologetic reasons, Josephus also probably suppressed those issues involving Israel alone in order to avoid offending his Roman audience. Thus Josephus's portrait of John makes him look like a good moral philosopher. Meier hints that the portrait of Luke 3:10–14 may connect with Josephus's portrait of John's ministry, pointing to a call for justice.

4. Mark (1:2) adds a connection to the idea of God's messenger sent ahead from Mal. 3:1, while Luke (3:6) lengthens the Isa. 40 citation to extend its outreach to all flesh (40:5), an emphasis fitting his concerns for non-Jews. These additions by the evangelists serve to introduce the ministry and give a context for its meaning.

similar to the Qumranians' call but without the focus on law or withdrawal; rather, his baptism represents an identification with the nation's and the individual's need to prepare for God's powerful coming. By submitting to baptism, one shared in the washing that the nation needed as preparation for God's coming. However, it was not the rite of washing that was key for John but the response of the heart ready for God to come. In fact, given Luke 3:10–14, the stress of John's call is that such a recognition of repentance will mean that the person prepared for God's coming will treat others with more compassion and integrity. There is an important dimension to John and Jesus's teaching that says turning toward God in repentance will impact how one also treats others. This is why, when Jesus is asked about the greatest commandment, he links love for God with love for one's neighbor. The two go together. How we love and worship God is seen by how we walk and love others.

As all the Synoptics make clear, there is a call to bear fruit worthy of repentance: this is a part of the call to be prepared and baptized. It represents the removal of obstacles that stand in the way of God's coming (cf. Isa. 57:14). Thus, there is a community dimension to the eschatological washing. When Jesus participates in John's baptism, he is identifying with and endorsing the message of the prophet, especially in its national dimension as a community statement of Israel's need for God and his coming.[5]

Associated with the baptism is the voice from heaven. This event appears to have been a primarily private interaction between Jesus and God, given Mark's description. However, John the Baptist apparently also had access to it as a witness for Jesus, as John's Gospel affirms (John 1:29–34). The other Gospels appear to highlight the event's significance. It was at this event that God marked out his beloved Son as his unique agent.

5. R. L. Webb, "Jesus' Baptism: Its Historicity and Implications," *Bulletin for Biblical Research* 10 (2000): 261–309. For discussion of issues tied to the historicity of John's baptism and ministry, as well as his baptism of Jesus, see R. L. Webb, "Jesus' Baptism by John: Its Historicity and Significance," in *Key Events in the Life of the Historical Jesus: A Collaborative Exploration of Context and Coherence*, ed. Darrell L. Bock and Robert L. Webb (Tübingen: Mohr Siebeck, 2009), 95–150; Darrell L. Bock, *Who Is Jesus? Linking the Historical Jesus with the Christ of Faith* (New York: Howard Books, 2012), 26–38.

Key to the event is not only the testimony of the heavenly voice but also the anointing by the Spirit. The voice marks out Jesus both as royal, given the allusion to Ps. 2:7, and as a servant figure, as the use of Isa. 42:1 shows. This affirmation lays the foundational groundwork for identifying Jesus's roles. The experience of the voice and God's provision of the Spirit served as a confirmation of his call. The anointing by the Spirit confirms the call by supplying the agent of enablement, who marks out Jesus as "anointed" (the Messiah-Christ) and also affirms his prophetic connection to the will of God.[6]

So we see God identifying Jesus as Son-Servant. Psalm 2 is a regal messianic psalm. Sonship and kingship come together, laying groundwork for what Jesus will say about the kingdom of God. What kind of son exactly is Jesus in relationship to the kingdom? What kind of servant is he exactly in relationship to the promise? The servant image looks to a figure who ultimately is not only God's messenger of deliverance but also one who will not be completely understood in that role, as Isa. 49:1–6 and 52:13–53:12 indicate. Most Jews had not anticipated the surprising juxtaposition of king and servant that will reveal the unusual features of Jesus's ministry. The unfolding of this combination is another part of the earth-up portrait the rest of the narratives will unfold.

With this directing call behind him, Jesus now is free to move out in ministry. He picks up the message where John the Baptist left off. God's rule is approaching in the one whom God has marked to take up the call. First, however, there is an important test of his readiness.

Jesus's Temptation: Introduction of the Battle Lines and the Son's Qualifications

All the Synoptics recount Jesus's temptations as the last event before Jesus moves into ministry. With Jesus's initial encounter involving a

6. Given the church's recognition of Jesus's divinity, such affirmation and confirmation may seem odd, especially primarily as a private experience. However, these acts represent an equipping that shows how seriously the Gospel writers took Jesus's humanity. His ministry has all the markings of, and more of the divine calling than, any major prophetic figure (cf. Isa. 6; Ezek. 1–3; Jer. 1). This is a part of the earth-up theme.

challenge by malevolent forces, the nature of a more cosmic battle for what Jesus's coming represents becomes a key part of the opening frame of Jesus's ministry. The battle is not with flesh and blood but with spiritual forces that seek to challenge the way and program of God.

Mark tells the account in summary form, simply stating that Jesus was tempted, was with the beasts, and had angels minister to him. Mark immediately follows the account with Jesus's proclamation that the time is fulfilled, the kingdom is approaching, and so one must repent and believe in the gospel. What is significant about Mark's version is that Jesus emerged unbowed from the test. Unlike a previous temptation (Gen. 3), there was no succumbing to the presence of evil.

Matthew and Luke give details, although in different order, with Matthew apparently giving the tighter sequencing. Matthew first narrates the devil's temptation for Jesus to turn stone into bread, then to dive off the temple's pinnacle, and finally to receive the kingdoms of the world by worshiping the tempter. Luke reverses sequence of the second and third temptations, making the temple challenge a climactic event, probably because of the importance of Jerusalem to the end of his Gospel, since he makes more of Jesus's journey to Jerusalem to meet his fate than do the other Gospels.

Both these writers use the event to precede the introduction of the Galilean ministry. Luke is most explicit when it comes to showing the importance of the event: he has the temptations follow a genealogy that ends with the identification of Adam as "son of God." Here is yet another sense in which "son of" is used. Son can picture the king, but also picture those made in God's image, created by him to walk with him and manage the creation. So Jesus succeeds where Adam failed and becomes the representative for humanity who is able to stand up to the devil. Where Matthew has Jesus qualified as Messiah to represent people, Luke has Jesus qualified as the reflection of humans made in the image of God.

So important themes of the temptations are Jesus's success and dependence on God, not to mention his qualifications to be a representative of Israel's hope and of humanity.

Also significant is the introduction of the devil as the key spiritual opponent to Jesus's cause. Opposition to Jesus is not merely or even primarily a matter of social or political forces. Jesus's later action in casting out demons will reinforce the point about the cosmic nature of opposition to Jesus. The event's uniform placement here before Jesus launches his ministry focuses on this "cosmic" dimension of Jesus's battle from the start. Jesus's call is to restore the creation. Some are out to stop it. That opposition is not merely or even primarily human. It is a battle of spirits that fight for the well-being and makeup of the cosmos.

Often it is claimed that the story of Jesus's temptation is a creation of the church. No doubt its explicit supernatural elements are responsible for such skepticism. The objection is raised that the event has no witnesses. But a better question might be, What would cause the church to remember such an event, whether in skeletal or detailed form, making it multiply attested in two strands of the church's tradition (Mark and Q [Q = material common to Matthew and Luke])? It seems that this had to be a story that Jesus related to his soon-to-be-gathered band of the Twelve. Its point would be to underscore that Jesus's mission was not ultimately just about politics or the social order. Rather, associated with Jesus's coming was a deeper spiritual battle in which unseen forces always seek to seduce people away from walking in the direction of God's call. Such a calling entailed suffering, not the kind of self-satisfaction that Satan was offering to the Son.

To precede the introduction of Jesus's ministry with this shared note means that the Synoptics have underscored where the real battle for hearts and souls lies, including choices between God and self. It is what Paul would stress later when he told the Ephesians that the believers' battle is not against "flesh and blood, but against the principalities, against the powers, against the world rulers of this present darkness, against the spiritual hosts of wickedness in the heavenly places" (Eph. 6:12).

Conclusion

These opening scenes strike many notes. Jesus is the one who advances the program of God and represents God taking up his promises anew. Covenant fulfillment is present. Notes of joy abound. A special birth launches the events. A king of the line of David arrives. God affirms Jesus's sonship through the bestowal of a call through the Spirit.

Yet evidence of resistance also appears. A leader bypasses the opportunity to welcome the child and instead brings suffering and murder. Mary is warned that events will cut through her heart like a sword. With Jesus's coming, dark clouds also appear. Satan shows up. Jesus eschews the opportunity to use his power on his own behalf. He will walk the path God gives to him. He will face the darkness as light, engaging the darkness as light.

2

Jesus's Central Message: The Kingdom of God

Sorting Out the Tensions in His Teaching

If you ask most Jesus scholars what idea was most central to Jesus's teaching, they will say it is the message he brought about the kingdom of God. The concept is interesting since the phrase does not come directly from the Hebrew Scriptures. It is more about an OT concept and hope that Jesus preached. Needless to say, a divine program about the kingdom has many issues and questions attached to its introduction as a central topic in Jesus's teaching. So we walk through many of these discussions in the next two chapters. First, one must define what the kingdom is about and consider the antecedents to the theme in the Hebrew Scriptures as well as in Second Temple Judaism. This will be done briefly. Then attention needs to be given to the apocalyptic character of kingdom hope and its promise of vindication and judgment. What is that hope? Is it a remake of this world, or is it a new world? Next to be considered is whether the kingdom is present, future, or both. The next chapter will then deal with the issue of realm. Is it spiritual, or is it tied to this earth, or is it both?

What we shall see is that many questions posed as a choice between understanding the kingdom in this way or in that way are actually a case of appreciating how both options are at work, with each context telling us whether one option or the combination is in view. Thus a survey of these discussions shows how broad and complex the theme of the kingdom is. Recognizing all the elements in these themes is important for appreciating all that is being said about the kingdom.

Program: The Kingdom of God as Expressing God's Dynamic Rule and Vindication of the Righteous Both Now and Yet to Come

Clearly, the kingdom is one of Jesus's most central teachings. A look at the use of the term for God's reign, βασιλεία, shows how deeply distributed the concept of kingdom of God/heaven is in the Gospels:

Mark (13×): 1:15 (//Matt. 4:17); 4:11 (//Matt. 13:11; Luke 8:10); 4:26; 4:30 (//Matt. 13:31; Luke 13:18); 9:1 (//Matt. 16:28; Luke 9:27); 9:47; 10:14 (//Matt. 19:14; Luke 18:16); 10:15 (//Luke 18:17); 10:23 (//Matt. 19:23; Luke 18:24); 10:24; 10:25 (//Matt. 19:24; Luke 18:25); 12:34; 14:25 (//Matt. 26:29; Luke 22:18). All but 4:26; 9:47; 10:24; and 12:34 have parallels in other Gospels, as shown.

Teaching material common to Matthew and Luke (i.e., Q; 9×): Matt. 5:3//Luke 6:20; Matt. 6:10//Luke 11:2; Matt. 6:33//Luke 12:31; Matt. 8:11//Luke 13:29; Matt. 10:7//Luke 10:9; Matt. 11:11//Luke 7:28; Matt. 11:12//Luke 16:16; Matt. 12:28//Luke 11:20; Matt. 13:33//Luke 13:20–21.

Matthew only (27×): 5:10, 19a, 19b, 20; 7:21; 8:12; 13:19, 24, 38, 43, 44, 45, 47, 52; 16:19; 18:1, 3, 4, 23; 19:12; 20:1; 21:31, 43; 22:2; 23:13; 24:14; 25:1.

Luke only (12×): 4:43; 9:60; 10:11; 12:32; 13:28; 17:20a, 20b, 21; 18:29; 21:31; 22:16, 18.

John (2 [or 3×]): 3:3, 5 (in 18:36 Jesus speaks of "my" kingdom).[1]

1. This list is adapted from Joachim Jeremias, *New Testament Theology*, trans. J. Bowden (London: SCM, 1971), 1:31. The above list adds the parallels to Mark.

John's use of the term "kingdom" shows just how multiply attested this theme is: the expression surfaces in every strand of the Gospel tradition.[2] Often it is said that John's concept of eternal life is his equivalent for the kingdom of God to make the idea more intelligible for a Greek audience.[3] In the Synoptics, Jesus did speak of entering life when one entered the kingdom, so the move fits with Jesus's teaching (Mark 9:43, 45; Matt. 7:14). So John's linkage of kingdom and eternal life makes sense. It also is clear that Matthew especially likes to report the phrase, while Luke is more restrained: Matthew has it thirty-two times as "kingdom of heaven" and four times as "kingdom of God" (Matt. 12:28; 19:24; 21:31, 43; a fifth use [Matt. 6:33] depends on a textual variant); Matthew has a reference in five places that Mark does not (Matt. 13:19; 18:1; 20:21; 21:43; 24:14), while Luke has it in three places where parallels with Mark lack it (Luke 4:43; 18:29; 21:31).[4] What does this key term mean? What are its antecedents? What other concepts in Jesus's teaching are tied to it? To make these key points of Jesus's teaching clear, we cover this term in some detail and subsume other key themes to it.

It is very rare for Matthew and Luke to drop a reference to the kingdom that is in Mark. Often, when it does happen, it is because of repetition with a previous line or a choice to omit a longer detail (e.g., Matt. 19:24 and Luke 18:24 lack the additional mention of "kingdom" found in Mark 10:24; Mark 10:15 and Luke 18:17 mention "kingdom" in a verse that Matt. 19 lacks altogether, though Matt. 18:3–4 is similar). One exception to this explanation is the lack of "kingdom" in Matt. 18:9 where Mark 9:47 has it, Matthew choosing instead to repeat "life."

2. This point about multiple attestation holds even if one prefers Matthean priority for the order of the Gospels.

3. Leonhard Goppelt, *Theology of the New Testament*, ed. Jürgen Roloff, trans. John E. Alsup (Grand Rapids: Eerdmans, 1981), 1:45.

4. Outside the Gospels, reference to the kingdom in this sense is rare: 14× in Paul (8× as kingdom of God), 8× in Acts, 5× in Revelation (2× as kingdom of Lord or God), twice in Hebrews, and once in James. This is not a common expression in the early church of the NT period. The tradition appears to treat it mostly as Jesus's speech. Matthew's use of "kingdom of heaven" appears to reflect Jewish reluctance to utter the term "God," to guard against breaking the third commandment: sometimes Jews used a euphemism for God rather than describe or invoke God directly. Examples include (1) how they spoke of the Lord as "Adonai" rather than use or read the name YHWH or (2) the use of dots in the manuscripts at Qumran where the name YHWH would otherwise appear. So "kingdom of God" is expressed as "kingdom of heaven," a respectful circumlocution for God.

Antecedents to the Term and Its Meaning: A Term with a Static Basic Meaning and Yet Variable Force

When Jesus used the phrase "kingdom of God," how much of its meaning can we assume he and his audience shared? This becomes an important question because the expression itself, surprisingly, is totally absent from the Hebrew Scriptures.[5] Here is a good example of where unpacking an idea involves more than the study of a specific phrase or term.

Although the expression "kingdom of God" is not present in the Hebrew Scriptures, the concept of God's promised rule is prominent.[6] Yahweh is king (1 Sam. 12:12; Ps. 24:10; Isa. 33:22; Zeph. 3:15; Zech. 14:16–17). He rules over Israel (Exod. 15:18; Num. 23:21; Deut. 33:5; Isa. 43:15). He rules over the earth or the creation (2 Kings 19:15; Isa. 6:5; Jer. 46:18; Pss. 29:10; 47:2; 93; 96:10; 145:11, 13). He possesses a royal throne (Pss. 9:4; 45:6; 47:8; Isa. 6:1; 66:1; Ezek. 1:26). His reign is ongoing (Pss. 10:16; 146:10; Isa. 24:23). Rule or kingship is his (Ps. 22:28). It is primarily God's special relationship to Israel that is in view in these texts, as the son of David is said to sit on Yahweh's throne (1 Chron. 17:14; 28:5; 29:23; 2 Chron. 9:8; 13:8). When Israel was overrun by the nations, a longing existed that one day God would reestablish his rule on behalf of his people and show his comprehensive sovereignty to all humanity. After all, God had committed himself to David, promising a dynasty of duration (2 Sam. 7:13). It is here that the hope of a future kingdom of God not made with hands came to be contrasted with human kingdoms in Dan. 2 and 7 (Dan. 4:3 alludes to the idea as a part of God's sovereignty over nations). In the context of such expectation Jesus used the expression "kingdom of God." What was hoped for was something that had existed in the past but only as a mere glimpse of what had been promised: a rule to come involving total peace for God's people. In sum, as a result

5. The expression does occur in Wis. 10:10.

6. Chrys C. Caragounis, "Kingdom of God/Kingdom of Heaven," *DJG*[1] 417. Avoiding the word/concept fallacy is key in doing good biblical theological work. We do not need to have a specific term to evoke a concept. Thus discussion of God's rule or reign can evoke the idea of God's kingdom without using the word "kingdom." The same in reverse is also true. When we raise the issue of God's kingdom, we are discussing some aspect of his ruling program.

of the Babylonian captivity, kingdom hope is driven forward by the vision of the fullness of God's rule appearing someday. It was to this hope that Jesus preached.

Such a hope had been nurtured in some circles of Second Temple Judaism.[7] The kingdom *could* be linked to the messianic hope, but it *always* was tied to the judgment of the nations and the vindication of the saints. Some Jewish documents, content with the current arrangement in the world, do not reflect any such hope. The theme is expressed with some variety, but central to its presence is that God will assert his comprehensive rule (*1 En.* 9.4–5; 12.3; 25; 27.3; 81.3). God's powerful presence will involve the removal of Satan's influence (*As. Mos.* 7–10). He will destroy his enemies and free his people. These enemies are described both in earthly terms, like the Romans (*Pss. Sol.* 17–18; *2 Bar.* 36–40), and in spiritual terms, as when Belial stands among the evil forces that will be defeated (1QS 3–4). Often the coming of the kingdom was seen as being preceded by a period of intense upheaval and tribulation (*Sib. Or.* 3.796–808; *2 Bar.* 70.2–8; *4 Ezra* [= 2 Esd.] 6:24; 9:1–12; 13:29–31; 1QM 12.9; 19.1–2). The cry of the prayer of 2 Macc. 1:24–29 summarizes well the hope of deliverance. The call was for God to deliver and vindicate his people. One passage (*Pss. Sol.* 17–18) gives the most detailed expression of messianic hope in all the texts, although the idea of kingdom in this period of Judaism did not always entail a messianic hope.[8] In fact, sometimes the messiah is seen in very earthly terms, as in the *Psalms of Solomon*, while in other texts, he clearly possesses a more transcendent power (*1 En.* 37–71) or seems to have a mix of the two (*4 Ezra* [= 2 Esd.] 7:28–29; 12:32–34; 13:26).

Thus, God's coming rule is preached as comprehensive and vindicating. God's rule for his people is a complex array of subthemes tied to the kingdom's coming. In Judaism, there was no unified view of the kingdom beyond the hope of God's powerful coming and vindication of the saints. That hope was expressed in a variety of ways,

7. Michael Lattke, "On the Jewish Background of the Synoptic Concept 'The Kingdom of God,'" in *The Kingdom of God*, ed. Bruce Chilton (Philadelphia: Fortress, 1984), 72–91.

8. Jacob Neusner, William Green, and E. Frerichs, eds., *Judaisms and Their Messiahs* (Cambridge: Cambridge University Press, 1987).

sometimes quite political, other times more spiritual. The messiah could be a political, national figure or a cosmic deliverer. Sometimes the nations were seen as being conquered, while other expressions of vindication hoped for the nations to be worshiping with Israel. It is important to appreciate how Jesus preached this hope into this somewhat confused backdrop. *There was no single Jewish hope for the kingdom other than sharing the idea that peace would come and the saints would be vindicated.*

This complex background raises questions: Could Jesus use the phrase "kingdom of God" and really be understood? More important, in presenting his understanding of the kingdom, could he assume that his audience would understand what he meant by invoking this idea? Given the absence of the exact phrase in the Hebrew Scriptures and the variety of details attached to the hope within Second Temple Judaism, Jesus needed to explain his usage in order to be clear.

This complexity raises the issue of whether Jesus's use of the expression was, as Norman Perrin posed, "static" (fixed) or "tensive" (variable).[9] Did Jesus use the expression one way all the time, with a fixed referent (static)? Or was his use of the expression something that he used with symbolic force but that could not be contained in one referent alone (tensive)? In contrast to Perrin's either-or option, a third possibility seems more likely: Jesus's use operates within a fixed parameter, which he filled with a variety of detail because of the richness of the basic concept that he was defining and detailing (tensive yet with a static-like base).[10] How one approaches Jesus's terminology will impact how one reads it.

9. This linguistic contrast was introduced by the later work of Norman Perrin, *Jesus and the Language of the Kingdom* (Philadelphia: Fortress, 1976), esp. 16–32, 127–31, 197–99. In discussing this point from Perrin, I highlight the linguistic element of his discussion without embracing his language about "myth" associated with the use of the expression "kingdom of God."

10. For an incisive critique of Perrin, see John Meier, *A Marginal Jew: Rethinking the Historical Jesus,* 2 vols., ABRL (New York: Doubleday, 1994), 2:241–43. He accuses the later Perrin of sounding like a twentieth-century Bultmannian as opposed to being attuned to a first-century Jew. Interestingly, the earlier Perrin made a similar critique about such a view of the kingdom. See Norman Perrin, *The Kingdom of God in the Teaching of Jesus* (Philadelphia: Westminster, 1963), 86, where he states, "A 'timeless' Kingdom is as foreign to 1st-century Judaism as a transcendent order beyond time and space, and if Jesus held such views he singularly failed to impress

Four factors favor this third option:

1. The number of, and variety within, the Gospel kingdom sayings placed alongside the absence of older direct references in the Hebrew Scriptures suggests that Jesus developed the OT kingdom along additional lines. However, Jesus's respect for what the Hebrew Bible taught means that he is not altering the concept but developing and complementing it. The variety within his kingdom teaching validates this point.
2. The very consistency of the fundamental image within Judaism means that a basic understanding of kingdom did exist on which Jesus could build. It is *God's* kingdom and rule that are presented as the hope. The sheer number of texts that discuss judgment and vindication under this theme both in OT Scripture and in later Judaism shows that Jesus works with a given understanding at its base. Reflection taking place within Second Temple Judaism represented attempts to put the hope of Scripture together in terms of the details. Jesus both accepts and rejects elements of these reflections.
3. The idea that Jesus works with a rarely used OT term and yet develops it by using larger categories of scriptural teaching has precedent elsewhere in his own use. Jesus does the same type of thing with the Son of Man concept. That description of a human invested with eschatological transcendent authority appears in Dan. 7 (note the conceptual overlap with the kingdom theme: Dan. 7 is a key kingdom text). Here one does not choose between the human and transcendent dimensions. Both are in play. Jesus takes this one image and uses it as a collection point for his christological self-understanding. In the same way, Jesus takes the kingdom concept and uses it as a collection point for both soteriology and eschatology.[11]

---

them upon his followers." In other words, the kingdom of God had a concreteness and materiality about it as a part of this earth and this history that prevented it from vaporizing into a vague kind of spiritual form of existence.

11. I suspect that the same premise operates with Jesus's use of "the law," but in the opposite direction. Here the term in question is so heavily used in the OT that Jesus's usage in any context must be carefully examined for its point and scope. One

4. The very confusion of detail within Judaism of Jesus's time demanded that he take this type of approach to the kingdom of God. Here was an expression that virtually did not exist in the OT. By Jesus's time, however, multiple concepts swirled around it, even though its basic meaning was well established. The expression clearly sought to summarize a major strand of Jewish hope, but it needed defining. Its absence from the OT gave Jesus room to make it a helpful synthesizing concept. Its familiarity and importance within Judaism, because of the hope it encapsulated, made it a key term to nail down. The very diversity in its contemporary usage required that Jesus explain and develop the term. Thus, as we turn to Jesus's usage, we can expect that he was referring to a hope that his audience understood in its most basic terms, yet an expectation that needed more detail and development.

So Jesus's use of the term "kingdom" is tensive yet has a stable base. In each of the categories we examine, it will be shown that Jesus's use is complex and must be examined one text at a time. Choices of either-or inevitably err in narrowing the depth of Jesus's usage. To make "kingdom" a static technical term for every use is to miss the variety of nuances in Jesus's usage within the stable, basic meaning. *The kingdom is about the presence of God's rule, the vindication of the righteous, and the judgment against God's enemies.* But what exactly does its coming involve? This raises the question of the kingdom as an apocalyptic theme.

Kingdom as an Apocalyptic, End-Time Theme: A Remaking of the World, a Renewing of This World in History, a Restoration for Israel, or All Three? Is It Coming Soon (Imminent)?

In considering Jesus's appeal to the kingdom, two questions dominate: (1) Did Jesus foresee (a) a divinely remade new world or (b) a

---

must know whether the law is being invoked because its stipulations are in view or because of its hope tied to promise. Where one (the law) might be seen to be coming to an end, with discontinuity highlighted, the other (the kingdom) is described in ways that point to continuity and hope. Again, one does not choose between the options and make everything continuity or discontinuity, but one must decide which angle is at work in a given context and recognize that all of them appear at one point or another.

divinely wrought reorganization of the current world, (c) including a role for Israel, or (d) possibly all of these?[12] (2) Did Jesus foresee that end (fulfillment), however conceived, as coming within his lifetime?

The difference in the OT between the prophetic-eschatological expectation and the apocalyptic-eschatological expectation highlights the problem as a debate between seeing a remade new age or an eschaton (final stage) within this history.[13] Prophetic hope is defined in terms of God's work within history, usually tied to God's raising up a royal figure who delivers Israel (e.g., Isa. 9). Apocalyptic hope is defined as God's powerful work manifesting itself in an inbreaking from outside into normal history (e.g., Dan. 7). Apocalyptic hope entails cosmic change, the introduction and presence of a transcendent-like figure, including the backdrop of an almost dualistic conflict with the cosmic forces of evil.[14] In sum, the Messiah represents prophetic-eschatological hope, while the "one like a son of man" represents apocalyptic-eschatological hope.

The interesting feature is that Jesus ties both strands together in his proclamation of the kingdom, though the more eschatological features seem to dominate outside the extensive usage of Jesus calling

12. The idea that Jesus did not have an apocalyptic hope, as made popular in the Jesus Seminar, is not likely. The most eloquent attempt to make this argument appears in the work of Marcus Borg, *Jesus in Contemporary Scholarship* (Valley Forge, PA: Trinity, 1994). For a critical assessment of this view, see Dale C. Allison Jr., *Jesus of Nazareth: Millenarian Prophet* (Minneapolis: Fortress, 1998), 96–129. The willingness of Jesus to be baptized by John argues that he agreed with John's message and call to Israel for reform in the face of prospective judgment.

13. For a summary of this distinction, see Paul D. Hanson, *The Dawn of Apocalyptic: The Historical and Sociological Roots of Jewish Apocalyptic Eschatology*, rev. ed. (Philadelphia: Fortress, 1979), 10–12; George Ladd, *The Presence of the Future* (Grand Rapids: Eerdmans, 1974), 45–101, esp. 79–83, 93–95. Unlike many of the discussions of this distinction, Ladd correctly sees something less than a clean differentiation between these categories, observing how the "apocalyptic" Daniel actually has many "prophetic" features. Ladd thus avoids the implicit tendency of many critics to pit the two approaches against each other. Given the "mix" in Daniel, the mix in Jesus's own presentation has precedent in the older Scripture.

14. Rather than appealing to a genre distinction, John Collins, *The Scepter and the Star: The Messiahs of the Dead Sea Scrolls and Other Ancient Literature*, ABRL (New York: Doubleday, 1995), 11–14, argues for a distinction in the form of the messianic expectation between a royal figure and a heavenly messianic figure. These are two of the four categories that he identifies in Judaism. The others are prophet and priest.

himself the Son of Man. The more apocalyptic features include the imagery of the Son of Man coming on the clouds, drawn directly from Dan. 7:13 (Mark 13:26 par.), along with the cosmic disturbances associated with his coming (Mark 13:24–25 par.).[15] Here is divine judgment crashing the earthly party down below, an inbreaking of God's authority. This imagery is significant because it is this return that brings judgment and allows the vindicated righteous to "inherit the kingdom" (Matt. 25:34). It involves the rule of God being expressed in its coercive fullness. Here God's kingdom and the returning Son of Man are linked. Judgment and vindication are standard Jewish apocalyptic themes of the kingdom, as we saw in treating the background to the concept. The images of a gathering up for a comprehensive judgment and of a bridegroom coming who shuts some out also have these overtones (Matt. 25:1–13, 31–46). The separation of the righteous from the unrighteous is the point of this imagery. Other elements in Jesus's teaching have a catastrophic, apocalyptic feel. These include the comparisons of the judgment with the flood (Luke 17:26–27; Matt. 24:37–39) and Sodom and Gomorrah (Luke 17:28–29). The Son of Man's sudden coming is compared to lightning, revealing the shock of the coming (Luke 17:24; Matt. 24:27).

Other images of the kingdom in the future are harder to classify in terms of this world or a remade world. The reversal of suffering or oppression, as reflected in the promises of the Beatitudes, could fit either emphasis, as do their hopes of reward (Matt. 5:3–10). The image of the rejoicing and fellowship at the banquet table also could belong in either scheme (Matt. 8:11–12; Luke 14:15–24; 22:16–18). One text seems to indicate that the plan still has Israel very much in view: the Twelve will judge "the twelve tribes of Israel" (Luke 22:30). In addition, the selection of the Twelve has been seen by many NT scholars as an indication that what Jesus was working for was a

15. I make this point against the view of Werner Kümmel, *Promise and Fulfillment: The Eschatological Message of Jesus* (London: SCM, 1957), 104. He splits the eschatological elements from the apocalyptic ones and argues that only the eschatological elements are authentic. Although Jesus's kingdom imagery is primarily eschatological, there is no inherent reason why the key turning point in the program should not be linked to apocalyptic imagery of God's decisive inbreaking, especially if Jesus saw himself in any sense as sent by God.

restoration of the nation, preparing them for the era of "regeneration" (Matt. 19:28 NKJV).[16]

Other texts also point to a future restoration for Israel. In Matt. 23:37–39 and Luke 13:34–35, Jesus declares the nation of Israel to be under an exilic-like judgment when he declares that their house is desolate. However, he sets a time limit by going on to declare, "until you say, 'Blessed is he who comes in the name of the Lord.'" This suggests the hope that the nation will eventually respond. The early church's continued hope for Israel points to an impetus from Jesus on the issue (Acts 1:6–7; 3:18–22; Rom. 9–11). That hope was described in terms that appealed back to the Hebrew Scriptures for what was to come, a hope in which not just the people but also the nation of Israel is prominent.

On the other hand, some teaching appears to shy away from the more overt apocalyptic themes of Judaism. Jesus specifically denies that signs accompany the time of the kingdom's appearing (Luke 17:20–21), although he does indicate that general signs exist in the age that should keep one watching. The issue of signs certainly is part of the Olivet Discourse of Mark 13; Matt. 24; and Luke 21. Such signs indicate that God is at work (Luke 12:54–56; Mark 13:1–37, esp. vv. 28–31). Jesus explicitly refuses to name an exact time for his return, precluding disciples from excessive calendrical calculating that often is tied to apocalyptic themes (Mark 13:32 par.). The commission of Acts 1:8, juxtaposed as it is to questions about the restoration of the kingdom to Israel, points to a call that is to be the focus of disciples, while the timing of all that comes with Jesus's return is seen as the Father's business.

Other texts are decidedly more eschatological and lack apocalyptic features. The parables of the sower, mustard seed, leaven, and tenants appear to place kingdom preaching and presence as having invaded this history, with no apocalyptic feel at all, operating more like a covert operation—so unnoticed that it is hardly appreciated as

16. Allison, *Jesus of Nazareth*, 101–2. Allison notes the parallels in Judaism that point in this direction: 1QM 2.1–3; 4QpIsa[d] frg. 1; *T. Jud.* 25.1–2; *T. Benj.* 10.7 (also Rev. 21:12). Scot McKnight, "Jesus and the Twelve," in *Key Events in the Life of the Historical Jesus: A Collaborative Exploration of Context and Coherence*, ed. Darrell L. Bock and Robert L. Webb (Tübingen: Mohr Siebeck, 2009), 181–214.

the presence of the kingdom program at all. Nevertheless, one day what has been started will reach a point of covering the whole world. These parables, explicitly presented as revealing a "mystery" (Mark 4:11//Matt. 13:11), show how Jesus's kingdom teaching spans more than a single catastrophic event or a given moment.

Here Jesus makes his distinctive contribution and goes in a fresh direction in comparison to previous Jewish expressions of kingdom hope. He apparently foresees a long-running program that was declared and initiated in his teaching and work but that will one day culminate in a comprehensive judgment. It is to this ultimate goal that the kingdom is headed. Thus the emphasis in the kingdom teaching of the Gospels is always aimed toward this fully restorative future. In this sense, Jesus's teaching is at one with the traditional Jewish hope. The emphasis explains why the disciples, after spending years listening to Jesus teach about the kingdom, could ask him after his resurrection if now was the time he was restoring the kingdom to Israel (Acts 1:6). Nothing in what Jesus had taught them had dissuaded them from this "national" dimension of the hope. And in equally characteristic style, Jesus replied neither with a time nor a date nor a correction but with an emphasis on the current call in light of that certain future.

The innovative feature in this teaching is that what the Hebrew Scriptures had presented as a package, Jesus developed in two phases, an inauguration of kingdom blessing of the Spirit and forgiveness, now to be given by him (Matt. 26:26–29; Mark 14:22–25; Luke 22:19–22; 24:49), and a later return with the full arrival of vindication, justice, and peace. This program in two phases meant that what Jews had expected to come all at once was delivered in a sequence that went from suffering rejection to exaltation.

The juxtaposition of these various prophetic and apocalyptic strands shows how eclectic and synthetic, even creative, Jesus's kingdom teaching is. Jesus did preach a hope that Jews could recognize, but his preaching went further. He embraced strands of Jewish apocalyptic hope but did not merely parrot these themes. The sense of these texts as a whole is that Jesus works within this history and yet also will reshape it one day. Again, the teaching is neither just this world reorganized nor a new world created, but both in their appropriate time. But how soon, O Lord, would this fullness come?

Three texts have dominated the discussion of Jesus's view of the imminent coming of the kingdom. Those who wish to credit Jesus with a view of imminence within a generation or so of his coming point to these three texts as decisive. On the other hand, one text within the Olivet Discourse warns us not to make a judgment before all the sayings are considered. The three "imminent" texts are Mark 9:1 (explaining that before some of the disciples die, they will see "the kingdom of God come in power" [AT]),[17] Matt. 10:23 (stating that before the disciples finish going "through all the cities of Israel," the Son of Man will come [CEB]), and Mark 13:30//Matt. 24:34 (arguing that "this generation will not pass away" until "all these things take place").

Mark 9:1 often is explained by appealing to the transfiguration as the event alluded to, a moment when the inner circle saw a sneak preview of Jesus's kingdom glory. Although objectors complain that Jesus would hardly refer to an event only six days or so hence against a time frame of the disciples' death, the fact is that only "some" did see this transfiguration glimpse of glory. But how the Gospels juxtapose this saying with the transfiguration commends this reading. That event as a foretaste of kingdom glory justifies its association with the kingdom of the end. There is no ultimate imminence foreseen in this passage.

The case for imminence surrounding Matt. 10:23 perhaps relies on an overly literal reading. The expression "go through all the cities of Israel" may mean nothing more than "completing your mission to Israel." In other words, they are to continue pursuing the nation until the Son of Man returns. When he does come, they still will be engaged in that calling. As we will see in a moment, this fits with something that Jesus says at Olivet. If this reading is correct, then neither is there imminence in this second of the three texts.

Mark 13:30//Matt. 24:34 is the most difficult saying. The initial impression that many gain from the text is that the events of the Olivet Discourse are predicted to happen by the end of "this generation," so the Son of Man's return is predicted within the disciples' lifetime.

17. Interestingly, the Matthean parallel in 16:28 has "before they see the Son of Man coming in his kingdom," again showing a link between Son of Man and kingdom.

However, as D. A. Carson has pointed out, to have the remark about this generation and "all these things" include the event of the return would contradict the earlier description that the coming will be like lightning, as well as not fit the preceding budding-leaf imagery of the Markan context.[18] In other words, the remarks about the Son of Man's appearing and the obvious cosmic signs that accompany it suggest that the event is excluded in the budding-leaf remark of the parable. The "leaf" remark describes the approach of the end, but not the culmination. This would mean that "all these things" refers to those events described before the arrival of the cosmic signs. Those events would happen within a generation, and that was just how it was, given that the fall of Jerusalem in AD 70 is a sign of the end and is a parallel to what the end itself would look like. The fall in AD 70, with the temple judgment, was a guarantee that the end also would come one day. The linkage to the AD 70 fall, without that being the end event, gives this discourse its sense of imminence.

Mark 13:10//Matt. 24:14 functions the same way as the Mark 13:30 "generation" text: Jesus did not teach that the fullness of the kingdom would come within the generation of the disciples. Here Jesus notes that before the end comes, "the gospel" (Mark), or "this gospel of the kingdom" (Matthew), will be preached in all the world. Thus a mission that would take some time seems to be in view in this remark. Another text, Luke 18:8, juxtaposes imminence with a long-enough delay that some will no longer have faith. This text reflects the tension in Jesus's teaching about his imminent return. Justice will come quickly yet is delayed to the point that some will not believe when the Son of Man returns.

So I argue that Jesus did draw on the apocalyptic-eschatological imagery of Judaism for his general portrait of the kingdom, but he also added new themes to that portrait. Jesus's teaching stressed where the kingdom was headed in the future. It would be a time when God would vindicate his people through the Son of Man and judge the nations. However, other texts hint that this is merely the end of a much longer story. Jesus refused to predict the time of the end, nor

18. See D. A. Carson, "Matthew," in *The Expositor's Bible Commentary*, ed. Frank E. Gaebelein (Grand Rapids: Zondervan, 1984), 8:506–7.

did he preach imminence in such a way as to declare that it would come within the generation of the disciples. Signs in their lifetime would and did indicate its approach, but the times and seasons for its coming were known only to the Father. The coming would be soon, and they were to keep alert as to its coming, but it would be long enough that some would no longer believe.

So Jesus's teaching had roots in Judaism and drew on both strands of Jewish teaching, one arguing that the kingdom would appear in history, and the other that it would remake the world. Interpreters often approach the kingdom as an either-or event, but the texts indicate that it is a both-and event. Jesus spoke of restoration *and* renewal. He did not sequence them. Jesus simply declared that this is what was coming. This was a fresh take and synthesis on Jewish kingdom teaching. But what else was fresh about his teaching? This brings us to the disputed topic of the timing of the kingdom's arrival.

The Kingdom's Coming: Present, Future, or Both?

C. H. Dodd's claim for a presently realized kingdom notwithstanding, the bulk of the references to the kingdom look to the future.[19] These Gospel passages treat the consummation of the kingdom, the final judgment, the coming of the Son of Man, the righteous being seated at the banquet table in an era of joy and fellowship, or a period to come when the kingdom is received, inherited, or prepared.[20] The kingdom that Jesus preached was a goal of God's promise and hope that brought deliverance and vindication through the working of God's power. But key to the ground for that golden age came through the ministry of one in whom and through whom God was and would be working. It is in this context that the issue of the kingdom's presence at the time of Jesus's earthly ministry must be raised. The kingdom

19. C. H. Dodd, *The Parables of the Kingdom*, rev. ed. (New York, Scribner, 1961).

20. Jeremias, *New Testament Theology*, 1:32–34, cites the variety of phrasing that occurs and notes how unique Jesus's teaching within Judaism is in showing such variety of expression. Bruce Chilton, *Pure Kingdom: Jesus' Vision of God* (Grand Rapids: Eerdmans, 1996), 56–101, lays out a summary of this entire teaching along a series of coordinates of themes: eschatology, transcendence, judgment, purity, and radiance. The listing shows the scope of major subtopics that the kingdom theme covers.

as future is clear in Jesus's teaching, but is there any sense in which it can be said to have begun?

On one point almost all are agreed: Jesus's message was about the kingdom. He preached the arrival of the eschatological age and its activity of deliverance, contrasting the greatness of the kingdom era with the era of the Baptist, which seemingly had now passed (Luke 4:16–30; 7:22–23, 28 par.; 16:16; Matt. 11:12–14).

Some texts highlight the kingdom's approach or proximity (Mark 1:15; Luke 10:9, 11).[21] The parable of the sower makes clear that the word about the kingdom is presently being sown, with the goal to bear fruit (Matt. 13:19). "The word" is compared to seed.

Other parables extend the image to include that of a mustard seed planted (Mark 4:30–32 par.). This is a crucial text that makes the imagery and timing tied to Jesus's teaching clear. At the start, it is a tiny seed, but it ends up as a tree in which birds can nest. This cannot be a reference to the comprehensive and consummative apocalyptic kingdom of the end, because that kingdom is decidedly great and comprehensive from its appearing with the Son of Man. Nor can it be a reference to the theocratic kingdom as seen in OT declarations of God's rule, because that cosmic, total rule also has been comprehensive from its inception.[22] What is in view here is the launching of the eschatological kingdom, which surprisingly is "breaking in" in minuscule form. So this parable is our first clue that a "mystery" of

21. Texts such as these make clear that whatever is being raised, it is not the universal kingdom of God, which declared God's rule in a generic sense or his rule over creation (e.g., Pss. 47; 96). The approach of the kingdom in Mark 1:15 and Matt. 4:17 looks to the arrival of something that has not been in place previously and that is longed for and anticipated. Thus any attempt to make present-kingdom texts in the NT fit into this more generic category in order to speak of Jesus teaching of only a future consummative eschatological kingdom fails. It is the promised eschatological kingdom that is drawing near. The generic kingdom that the OT, and especially the Psalter, declares as present is part of God's sovereign rule as Creator, but the eschatological kingdom that John and Jesus announce as arriving is the eschatological kingdom program tied to deliverance and restoration in a creation in need of renewal.

22. In a sense, the coming of the promised eschatological kingdom makes visible the universal rule that God always possesses in a way that leaves no doubt that he rules. Thus what the "theocratic" OT texts declare will become indisputably obvious when the promised kingdom comes. In a sense it is a fusion of kingdom horizons, where God's role as Creator is matched by what he has accomplished in deliverance.

the kingdom involves its seemingly insignificant start in the present. Jesus's announcement of its coming and his ministry are like seed going into the ground on its behalf, pointing to its inception. The parable of the leaven (Matt. 13:33) makes the same point in distinct imagery.

Equally suggestive about the significance of Jesus's activity for the kingdom's presence during his ministry are the images of Jesus as a bridegroom (Mark 2:18–22 par.), a shepherd (Matt. 9:36 par.; 10:6; Luke 12:32 [cf. Ezek. 34]), and a harvester sending messengers out to reap the harvest (Matt. 9:37–38; Luke 10:1–2), all of which are eschatological images. All of this suggests that if the kingdom has not come, it is very, very close.

Notice how these texts permeate all the Synoptic Gospels. The kingdom is so close that the disciples are experiencing what previous generations anticipated and hoped for. Jesus's announcement was a clear allusion to the arrival of the hoped-for promise that those in the past only anticipated (Luke 10:23–24 par.). For example, the offer of forgiveness that Jesus declares presents one of the great hoped-for blessings of the new era (Jer. 31:31–33; Mark 2:5; Luke 7:36–50; 19:1–10). For another example, the arrival of the Spirit is part of the current blessing that John the Baptist and Jesus both taught would come (Luke 3:15–17; 24:49, in a context where Hebrew Scripture hope has been invoked).

At the center of all of this activity was Jesus. That Jesus could interpret Torah and even explain its scope so that religious practice could change pointed to the arrival of a new era, a new way of administering blessing, a dispensation where the Spirit is writ large on the heart (Matt. 5:21–48; Mark 7:1–23; John 3:3–9; 4:20–25). It is true that not all the texts cited mention the term "kingdom," but most do. Nonetheless, the concepts and imagery speak to the era of eschatological promise, deliverance, and renewal, which is at the heart of kingdom hope. The other texts that do not use the term are describing the delivering and teaching activity of the one through whom the hoped-for promise comes. So one is still in the sphere of discussing the hoped-for kingdom. In Judaism, the kingdom was about the age to come or the messianic era. Remember that in the Hebrew Scriptures, the precise expression "kingdom of God" does not appear, though it is the actual topic of many other related themes. So the work of the Messiah qualifies as kingdom work of the promised era, especially given teaching in the parables that the kingdom is being planted in Jesus's teaching. The fact that this teaching is "new" or a "mystery" does not alter the fact that it is kingdom teaching connected to the original promise about the kingdom. So mystery, even where it brings fresh teaching about the kingdom in relationship to the OT, comes in alongside the promises of old to complete and complement what God had already revealed. This is why when the early church preached these themes in Acts, the note struck was that the completion of promise that Jews had always hoped for was being offered in what Jesus had done and in what he still had left to do (Luke 24:44–47; Acts 2:16–39; 3:13–26).

In some texts of Jesus's teaching, the kingdom also comes now, not just later. That the kingdom is not delayed because of Israel's rejection is shown in the parable of the great banquet (Luke 14:15–24). Here, the refusal by invitees to come to the celebration when it is announced does not lead to a postponement of the banquet but to an invitation extended to others to attend. Although banquet imagery is normally looking to the future in Jesus's teaching, in this case his preaching and the invitation to experience blessing starting now are in view. Those who turn their backs on the invitation are those rejecting Jesus at the current time he is ministering. They are missing the time to enter in and celebrate what God is doing. They are missing the fellowship that comes from being at the table with God, something also shown by the imagery of the Last Supper and of the Lord's Table, which grew out of the Last Supper. These texts mean that the heart of the kingdom is the mediation of promised blessing and deliverance, an exercise of divine power, and authority through a chosen, anointed one, who also acts with unique authority.

Among texts that talk about the presence of the kingdom, however, two stand out: Matt. 12:28//Luke 11:20; and Luke 17:21. It is in these texts that two key elements of the kingdom surface, one already made obvious by our survey, the other focusing on a key element that makes deliverance possible.

In Luke 17:20–21 Jesus declares that one need not go on a search for signs to find the kingdom. This reinforces a point that he has already raised in his teaching through the rebuke about being able to read the signs of the weather but not the signs of the times (Luke 12:54–56 par.). It also parallels the warning about the sign of his preaching being the only sign that this wicked generation will have to respond to (Luke 11:29–32 par.). The kingdom does not come, in this current phase, with such heavenly portents; rather, it is "in your midst." The correct rendering surely is not "within you," even though this was a common rendering long ago in many versions including the KJV, ASV, and NIV 1984.[23] Although linguistically ἐντός can have such a meaning and most often does, Jesus is not speaking of some potential within each person's heart to establish the kingdom. This reading sounds like the now mostly discredited romantic notions of nineteenth-century scholars on the kingdom in which Jesus's work was basically one that changed hearts in a strictly individualized way. This personalized reading is highly unlikely because Jesus's audience here is made up of Pharisees. Such heart potential for them does not exist without God's powerful work and the effect of his transforming presence through the Spirit, which comes only with a response of faith or belief in Jesus's message. Nor is the kingdom fundamentally so individualized; rather, it is a community to which one belongs.

The point of the expression is best rendered "in your midst" or "in your grasp." Jesus is making the point that one need not look for signs, because the kingdom is present among them in him. In Jesus, the kingdom, in a sense, is right in front of their faces. The object of the hunt for that which represents the kingdom's presence and authority stands before them.[24] That Jesus is speaking of the

23. I also reject the reading of Caragounis ("Kingdom," 423–24), who argues for a reading of "within you" as a basic expression of the kingdom's internal, dynamic character without requiring that it refer directly to the Pharisees. Such a reading ignores whom Jesus is addressing in the context and therefore is not likely. For the linguistic elements of the debate, see the next note below.

24. On the question of whether Greek papyri and other texts evidence a meaning of "among" for ἐντός, see Kümmel, *Promise and Fulfillment*, 33–36, esp. n. 50. This evidence—texts from Xenophon (*Anabasis* 1.10.3), Herodotus (*Histories* 7.100.3), and Symmachus's translation of Ps. 87:6—challenges Caragounis's claim of the absence of such attestation. Kümmel argues that an objection based on the audience being the Pharisees is not persuasive in arguing against "within you," because we cannot be sure that they are the original audience for this saying. I do not share his

present and not the future becomes clear when the present tense of Luke 17:21 is contrasted with the future perspective of verses 22–37. Such a reading highlights how Jesus is placed at the hub of kingdom activity, fitting all the other themes of realized promise pointing to Jesus's centrality. The text as a whole running to verse 37 shows the very already–not yet dimension so central to Jesus's teaching on the kingdom. The kingdom is arriving, is here, and yet is still to come in fullness. It is invading the world that so desperately needs God's restorative touch.

In the second text, Matt. 12:28//Luke 11:20, Jesus is defending himself against the charge that he casts out demons by the power of Beelzebul. He replies, "If I cast out demons by the Spirit of God [Matthew] / finger of God [Luke], then the kingdom of God has come upon [ἔφθασεν] you" (NASB). Is Jesus noting that the kingdom has come close to overtaking them or that it has come?

The key here is the aorist form of the verb φθάνω (Matt. 12:28// Luke 11:20). It appears in the Gospels only in this passage. In 1 Thess. 4:15 it means "to precede." However, in all its other aorist uses, it has the meaning of "has arrived" or "has reached" (Rom. 9:31; 2 Cor. 10:14; 1 Thess. 2:16; Phil. 3:16). It is not synonymous with the earlier declaration that the kingdom of God "has drawn near" (ἤγγικεν).[25] It says more than that the kingdom is near. The phrase "has drawn near" speaks of the kingdom's approach, but the idea that the kingdom has come emphasizes the inbreaking of the kingdom. It is here and is here to stay. It is alive on arrival.

Contextually, a real exercise of divine power is visibly present. The image is reinforced immediately in both contexts by the parable of a stronger man overcoming a strong man and plundering his possessions. Jesus is describing what happens when an exorcism or a healing takes place, not what is approaching. The point is that the miracles are a picture of God's authority and rule working through Jesus to defeat Satan. There is a reversal of fortune in the creation, a

skepticism about the setting. Such a challenge to Jesus's opponents fits nicely with many other such challenges pointing to Jesus's centrality in God's work. See also Meier, *A Marginal Jew*, 2:412–23, who defends the authenticity of the saying and discusses its likely Aramaic form.

25. Again, for details, see Kümmel, *Promise and Fulfillment*, 105–7.

hope expressed in Jewish texts (like *As. Mos.* 10.1).[26] In other words, the Jewish claim that Jesus does miracles by the satanic authority of Beelzebul could not be more incorrect.

This saying is significant for a series of reasons. First, it shows that the kingdom is about divine deliverance through Jesus. His releasing of authority overcomes Satan's presence and influence. It is an invasion of a realm that this evil one seemingly controls. Jesus is able to exercise such authority now. Jesus's ministry means that Satan already is being defeated. The arrival of the kingdom's presence in power is evident. His work of restoration involves power points. Jesus is stronger than the one (Satan) who is in the world. Although the kingdom ultimately includes a much more comprehensive exercise of power, as the future kingdom sayings show, it is operative now in the work of deliverance that Jesus's miracles reflect.

A second important point also is made through Jesus's miracles. The miracles themselves are not the point, but what they show. A study of Jesus's ministry shows how he worked hard to deflect excessive attention from his miracles. The miracles were "signs," as the Johannine perspective argues. They painted in audiovisual terms the presence of Jesus's authority and victory over Satan. They testified to the authority that Jesus brings. Such power had to be exercised and established for deliverance to take place.

So there emerges a third point from Jesus's exorcisms. This passage shows the injection of an apocalyptic theme again into Jesus's kingdom teaching. The kingdom manifests itself as part of a cosmic battle, expressed in dualistic terms, in which God through Jesus is defeating Satan, who himself is doing all he can to keep humanity opposed to God. These miracles show what is going on in the normally unseen cosmic and spiritual world. The apocalyptic dualism discloses what is going on in the world beyond what our five senses could normally perceive. With the coming of Jesus and the kingdom inaugurated, eschatology has entered into the present. Future hope dawns as present reality, but with much more reality to come.

26. To show this theme is the burden of the full article by Craig Evans, "Exorcisms and the Kingdom: Inaugurating the Kingdom of God and Defeating the Kingdom of Satan," in Bock and Webb, *Key Events in the Life of the Historical Jesus*, 151–79.

The summary of the miracle also reveals its importance. It is a combined miracle and pronouncement account. However, it is unlike most miracle accounts, which spend most of their time on the details of the miracle and little time on the reaction. This account gives only one verse to the healing (Matt. 12:22//Luke 11:14) and then spends all its time on the reaction (Matt. 12:23–32//Luke 11:15–23). Unlike other miracle stories, this miracle account emphasizes the result rather than the actual healing. That developed section on the reaction presents a commentary on the significance of Jesus's miracles as a unit. So the text is not just about this one miracle but especially about what the miracles as an entire feature of Jesus's ministry shows. What emerges is that the kingdom ultimately is about God's work to redeem humanity according to his promise. In a world needing restoration and renewal, the kingdom is God's ultimate response to the grip that Satan has on a needy people. The kingdom's coming in Jesus's ministry is the inaugurating of that reversal and a manifesting of that delivering power. So the miracles per se are not the point; instead, they serve as evidence for, and as illustrations of, a far more comprehensive deliverance that one day will extend across the entire creation. That is in part why the preaching about the kingdom was also called "good news." Jesus's ministry proclaimed and presented a kingdom hope. That hope had made an appearance through Jesus in his exercise of divine power, which served as a kind of cosmic email and invitation to share in what God was doing through this chosen one.

So the kingdom teaching of Jesus involved declarations about both his present ministry and the future tied to it. A kingdom long viewed as strictly future and greatly anticipated was being pulled into the present and made initially available in an exercise of comprehensive redemptive power. This display showed that the struggle was not merely with flesh and blood but also with principalities and powers. His kingdom, again to use the language of John's Gospel, was "not of this world" (John 18:36), although it was breaking into this world and in many ways introducing something new in stages. Although it would come in comprehensive power one day, in Jesus's ministry it was also invading now. Humanity could experience that victory over Satan both now and in the age to come.

As has already been noted, this splitting up of the program into a now phase and a not-yet phase is another fresh feature of what Jesus was doing. In a sense, in terms of past expectation, the program was being stretched out. Rather than coming all at once, the program of promise was realized in stages.

All of this explains a remark that John the Baptist made about "the stronger one to come" (AT). Though the remark does not directly invoke kingdom imagery, it does invoke messianic imagery and is a part of a ministry whereby John was preparing people for the coming of the Lord and the kingdom's approach. How would one know that the Messiah had come (and thus that this kingdom promise was arriving)? Luke 3:15–17 answers the question uniquely, even though Luke shares much of the passage with the Synoptics. For only Luke tells us that John explained how he was not the Christ at a time when people were contemplating whether he might be the Christ (Luke 3:15). The Baptist explains that he is not the Christ, but that the Christ's coming would be marked out by a baptism different from his own, one not with water but with Spirit and fire (Luke 3:16–17//Matt. 3:11–12).

In effect, John was explaining how one could know that the new era had come and how one could recognize that the longed-for Christ had arrived. John explained that the new era would be marked by a dispensing of the Spirit, a dispersal of enablement, and a mark of incorporation into the redeemed community of God. The kingdom ultimately is future, but its formation began with the powerful preaching and work of Jesus, drawing citizens to the new rule that he was in the process of establishing from within and among people. It had both individual and corporate elements. Each person needed to respond to the kingdom, and yet the kingdom bound those who responded to each other. The good news of the kingdom's arrival was about a new provision for a new people in an inbreaking new world. That community was called to be a preview of something God would eventually do in fullness later. But with forgiveness and the Spirit, the new era had made its debut. Again, we are not forced to choose whether the kingdom is now or not yet. Here is yet another kingdom truth that is not an either-or but a both-and.

So if the kingdom was arriving, then where exactly was the kingdom to be found? Whom did it include? This raises another debated aspect of Jesus's kingdom teaching: Is the kingdom about a divine dynamic presence lacking a specific sphere or realm? Or does it have a locale? In the next chapter, we turn our attention to yet another topic often posed as an either-or, an important subtheme for understanding the reality of the kingdom.

3

The Nature of the Kingdom: Presence, Realm, Ethics, Messiah, and the Father

Key Elements of the Kingdom Puzzle

The texts covered in the previous chapter made clear that the presence of the kingdom can be defined in terms of the dynamic or active presence of God's power and authority. God's rule is expressed as the exercise of his authority. The miracles depict Jesus's defeat of Satan via the power points that are signs of the kingdom's arrival (Luke 11:20; Matt. 12:28). Thus Jesus's miracles show the inbreaking of God's authority, the presence of his power. The kingdom's bringing the Spirit to indwell believers as a result of forgiveness of sins also reflects this dimension of kingdom activity (Matt. 26:26–29; Mark 14:22–25; Luke 3:16; 22:19–20; 24:49).

Jesus's presence as God's unique delivering representative means that the kingdom also is present. The promised mediation of the Spirit through Jesus is evidence of the presence of this rule and the new era's arrival, since the giving of the Spirit is a key messianic work

(Acts 1:8). The arrival of Spirit enablement, indwelling, and direction is very much the point of what makes Jesus's kingdom message good news. This idea is not as explicit in the Gospel material, but it is there and also appears more emphatically in Acts and the Epistles.[1] Most NT scholars accept this "dynamic" element as central to Jesus's teaching,[2] but there is more debate over the issue of realm.[3] This problem is exceedingly complex because once again Jesus makes the point in a variety of contexts through an array of themes.

First, several texts indicate that Israel or activity associated with Israel is an important element in kingdom teaching. I have already noted that the choosing of the Twelve (Matt. 10:2–4 par.) and Jesus's remark about the disciples sitting on the twelve thrones over Israel (Matt. 19:28–30 par.) indicate that they will have some position of judgment in the kingdom. Other texts indicate that the disciples, after hearing all of Jesus's teaching, still expected a role for the nation of Israel. Acts 1:6 describes the disciples asking if Jesus will now be restoring the kingdom to Israel. Jesus, though he does not directly answer the question of when, does not reject the premise of the question. In fact, two chapters later, in Acts 3:21, Peter states that at his return, Jesus will bring "the time of universal restoration" (NRSV)—a kingdom theme already described in the Scripture.[4] Thus

1. I have developed this idea of what the gospel is in the NT in a biblical-theological study of this theme in the Bible; see Darrell L. Bock, *Recovering the Real Lost Gospel: Reclaiming the Gospel as Good News* (Nashville: B&H, 2010).

2. A key work that argues for this emphasis is Bruce Chilton, *God in Strength: Jesus' Announcement of the Kingdom*, SNTSU 1 (Freistadt: Plöchl, 1979).

3. Older dispensational writers often say that George Ladd denied the presence of an idea of realm in Jesus's teaching because Ladd highlighted the dynamic force. But this characterization is wrong. Ladd simply argued that the dynamic sense was the more prevalent idea in the sayings. See George Ladd, *The Presence of the Future* (Grand Rapids: Eerdmans, 1974), 195–205.

4. Texts like these preclude any appeal to a "sociology of knowledge" as a way of saying that the prophets were limited in what language they could use to express what later developed in their expression of hope. Not only does this sociology view seem to affirm that the OT does not mean what it appeared to mean at the time it was given, but also one can ask, Why limit such a hermeneutical category to the OT? A denial of such an appeal means that Israel is a reference to national Israel in such texts. As a result, God's commitment to them is affirmed in such texts. Speaking of Acts 1:7, Craig Keener (*Acts: An Exegetical Commentary*, vol. 1, *Introduction and Acts 1:1–2:47* [Grand Rapids: Baker Academic, 2012], 687) asserts: "Contrary to the later Gentile church's de-Judaized way of reading Scripture, Jesus does not

the eschatological dimensions of the kingdom hope emerging from the OT seem to be affirmed in this Spirit-inspired speech.

Second are texts associated with the celebratory-banquet imagery. These point to an end-time victory and a shared, corporate place where the celebration occurs. At the Last Supper, Jesus refuses the final cup of wine and declares that he will not partake of the Passover again until he does so in the context of fulfillment in the kingdom (Luke 22:16–18). Thus Jesus looks forward to a day when the celebration will commemorate the completion of promise rooted in OT expression. Whatever additional elements there are to the kingdom realm (and there are additional elements, as we will see), they do not preclude an element involving the old Israelite expression of hope.

Third are texts suggesting the language of gathering that includes ethnic Israel but also looks beyond Israel. Luke 13:28–29 looks to people coming from "east and west" to sit at the table with the patriarchs. My only point here is that this is standard Jewish imagery.[5] Matthew 8:11–12, the parallel, suggests that the surprising inclusion of Gentiles is in view but not the entire exclusion of Israel. After all, the disciples represented a remnant of the nation. In other words, Gentile inclusion does not mean Israelite exclusion.

Fourth are a key set of texts in Matt. 11:12 and Luke 16:16. Many treat these as parallels and point to the Matthean conflict imagery of people seeking to take the kingdom by violence as key to both texts.[6] My own suspicion is that Luke does not parallel Matthew's conflict

---

deny that Israel's restoration will come." In response to the claim that the disciples' question is shortsighted and missed Jesus's point, Keener says that "the problem is with timing (Acts 1:7), not with content" (ibid., 683). In other words, the disciples ask a right question when asking about restoration of the kingdom to Israel. Jesus's reply is that the timing is the Father's business, not theirs. Jesus does not reject the premise of the question.

5. See Dale C. Allison Jr., *Jesus of Nazareth: Millenarian Prophet* (Minneapolis: Fortress, 1998), 141–43, although he dismisses the significance of the Matthean context too easily and thus denies a Gentile dimension to this image.

6. In Matt. 11:12 I have in mind the second half of the verse, where people are contending over the kingdom, part of the battle motif. In the first half of the verse, the reference to βιάζεται is disputed. It refers either to the kingdom suffering violence, a reading that matches the latter half of the verse, or to the kingdom advancing. Even if the idea of advance is present, it probably still refers to the inbreaking of the kingdom moving into the world, as opposed to the idea of a continuously ascending advance.

imagery here but instead points to the persuasion of preaching in his version of the image. However, this exegetical debate does not alter the key point here: the kingdom is a "thing" or a place contended over (or preached about), even in the present.[7] The image is of a realm introduced into the world as an object of contention (and discussion) within it.[8]

Fifth is a new category of realm tied to the kingdom, a place associated with paradise and extending beyond this world. It appears in Luke 23:42–43. Here the thief on the cross asks to be remembered when Jesus comes into his kingdom. The request, understood in normal Jewish terms, looks to the future. Jesus's reply brings the future into the present yet again when he tells the thief that this very day he will be with Jesus in paradise. Although the reply does not use the term "kingdom," the idea of paradise is a part of that hope in Judaism. When it comes to the issue of death, there is a sense in which Jesus reveals a current cosmic claim and dimension to the kingdom, authority over life and death. Death is a realm and also extends beyond Israel, even beyond this earth, but it is a part of the creation where God redeems. This appears to be another fresh dimension to Jesus's teaching.

Sixth, there is the host of texts looking to the judgment of the end, where the Son of Man carries out the eschatological assessment of humanity. In one sense this is the natural extension of the previous category. I highlight one dimension of one text, the Matthean parable of the wheat and the darnel (Matt. 13:24–30, 36–43). Here Jesus explains that the field is "the world." In that world, good seed has been sown, but the evil one also has sown what has come up as "weeds." All of this describes ongoing kingdom activity across the entire world and over all of humanity to the point of consummation. Jesus will not sort out grain from weeds until the "end of the age." My point here is that the kingdom, though present in the positive,

7. Darrell L. Bock, *Luke 9:51–24:53*, BECNT (Grand Rapids: Baker, 1996), 1351–54.

8. In the NT, texts like Acts 8:12–14, which juxtapose preaching about the kingdom, Jesus, and the word of God (= the word about the gospel of salvation in Jesus), show that the early church made this point (also Acts 19:8; 28:23, 30–31). Colossians 1:12–14 is similar in thrust.

visible, wheat-bearing activity of the seed sown by the Son of Man (i.e., Jesus) among believers, also makes a claim on all humanity, a claim for which each person will be accountable in the judgment at the end. In the world one either comes up as wheat or weed, and the Son of Man deals with both: he commands the weeds to be burned and the wheat to be stored.

Thus there is an aspect of the realm of the kingdom that extends beyond the believing people of God and makes a claim on all humanity in the world, even from the time of the present "sowing" (i.e., preaching) of the kingdom.[9] Regardless of whether people recognize it, the kingdom interpenetrates the world. The preaching of the gospel and its claim on all people emerge from imagery like this. God sorts everything out in the end, and no one is excluded from that evaluation in judgment.

Thus in terms of realm, the kingdom operates at several levels at once, depending on the context. In terms of its comprehensive presence, the realm looks to the future and the comprehensive establishment of peace and fellowship after a purging judgment. This realm appears to include hopes of old from Israel, yet it also looks to far more: a comprehensive exercise of authority over the whole of creation, including the blessing of many from outside Israel.

However, there is also a sense in which we can talk about a realm in the present.

1. An operative but invisible realm is at work in the community that Jesus is forming, as the power and presence of God is at work among those "sown by the Son of Man." I call it an "invisible" realm because, as the rest of the NT indicates, it is a power of God working during Jesus's absence through the Spirit in those who believe and in anticipation of his visible return and rule. It also works outside of human political structures. It is its own

9. In other words, this text is not about some people professing Christendom within what became the church but about the Word's work in the world and claim upon the world through his preached word. Jesus's judgment will cover all people, not just those in the church or those who profess to belong to it. As such, the scope of this text goes beyond any professed Christendom. The field, as Jesus makes clear, is the world, not something that he has gathered out of it.

multiethnic community that is mixed in among the nations and is distinct from them. It is the community that recognizes and responds to Jesus as Lord, Son of Man, Christ. It is the place where he is head, what the epistles will call the church or the body of Christ (Eph. 1:22; 5:23).

Here, in this outworking of the Spirit, the kingdom of God is especially at work, creating sacred space within the fallen world and its larger public space. Believers are called to live in that larger public space (as diverse, mixed with good and bad fruit, and fallen as public space is). Yet these believers are to reflect sacred power in the way they engage with the world and in the particular way they show real community among themselves. In doing so, they are to invite those outside in the world into the sacred space of the operative kingdom. Failure to see this distinction can lead to an assumption that the world is, or is to be, the kingdom, rather than seeing the kingdom as breaking into the world, interspersed within it and transcending national or ethnic identity. The transforming work of God is to be seen most evidently in the new community God has formed in the midst of the world. This is why Jesus spoke so little of Roman politics and chose to undermine it in the formation of a different kind of community in Rome's midst. Missing the distinction between public and sacred space helps to explain why Jesus spoke of rendering to Caesar the things that are his and rendering to God the things that belong to the deity. It also defines the mission of the kingdom today as focusing on its own spiritual integrity as it engages the world in a call to enter into the sacred space God creates as a counter to the world and its ways. Cultural mandates that ignore this distinction miss a key way in which God seeks to impact society. The creation of a kingdom in the midst of a fallen world is a primary way God works to bring change in the world. The difference between operative kingdom presence and power and the world in the era before the consummation is an important distinctive in Jesus's kingdom teaching.

2. Nevertheless there is also a "claimed realm" in that the kingdom issues a claim on the entirety of humanity in anticipation of the

> eventual scope of God's redemptive presence.[10] This claim is the foundation for the judgment to come. It justifies extending the gospel of the authoritative Jesus to every tribe and nation. It entails every person's accountability before the one true God and his chosen one, so that there is only one way to God. Both in the visible presence of God's authority in the community being transformed by the work of the Spirit and in the claimed presence of divine authority in the challenge to all to respond to God, the future is pulled into the present by the preaching, presence, and challenge of the Son of Man. Responding positively to him brings one into this new realm, though in other contexts one can speak of entering or inheriting this kingdom later, when it is ultimately fully realized. The one who is born again enters into this new way of relating to God in the way God designed (John 3:3–9). The exceptional text with the penitent thief on the cross shows that ultimately what is at stake is eternal presence and fellowship with God in unending and renewed life. The entry into paradise for the thief that day represents another foretaste of the ultimate, comprehensive victory to come that will be the kingdom "fully and coercively" present, a hope that the majority of kingdom texts in the Gospels affirm when they depict the consummation of kingdom hope that will cover the entirety of the creation.

Thus the kingdom is about the powerful and even transforming presence of God's rule through Christ. That rule is expressed today in the community of those whom he "planted," what became the church. But the kingdom is bigger than the church. The kingdom's presence now is but a precursor to a more substantial presence in the future. Jesus will redeem or judge what is being claimed now. In the end, the authority of the Son of Man will judge humanity and bless those who sit with him at the table. Then the kingdom will fully show itself with traits that the Scriptures of Israel had long promised. The

10. Here my reading does not limit the authority to "Christendom." The claim is far more comprehensive in scope than this. The weeds in the world are a reference not to professing Christians but to humanity at large in the world, including those outside the sown word that Jesus brings.

full features of rule will bring justice, peace, and righteousness to the creation. The kingdom "anticipated now in Spirit transformation" and "fully and coercively" present in the future summarizes the two ways the issue of realm is treated in kingdom texts. These kingdom texts treat as realms Israel, the church, the world, and the creation as a whole; which realm is being considered varies with each particular passage. Inclusion of Gentiles does not mean exclusion of Israel. Spiritual presence with Jesus, even through death now, does not preclude the coming of peace to the earth later, nor does it limit to whom it may come. Gentile presence in blessing as equal beneficiaries in the grace of God in the present does not mean that hope for Israel is excluded in the future. Here the "tensive" character of the term "kingdom" becomes obvious. There is much more to come in the kingdom program. The rest of the NT does much to fill in the details of what is outlined here in Jesus's teaching, especially in the eschatological texts of Paul's Epistles and in the book of Revelation: Jesus's teaching set certain trajectories for kingdom instruction that the rest of NT revelation develops and in some cases builds upon beyond what Jesus taught. This is why one cannot simply appeal to what Jesus taught as the only guide to what the NT teaches about the end. What Jesus provides is more of a hub of themes that the rest of the NT revelation develops. So is the kingdom about dynamic presence or a particular realm or place of rule? Once again a question often posed as either-or shows itself to be both-and.

In the Gospels, one final issue remains: the connection between righteousness and the kingdom, or what has been called the kingdom and ethics. It is to this topic that we now turn.

Kingdom and Ethics

In the end, the transformation associated with the inbreaking of the kingdom is not merely an abstract exercise in theology or definition. It is designed to impact life, both now and later. Thus the connection between kingdom and living or kingdom and ethics needs attention.[11]

11. This section is indebted to four studies: Norman Perrin, *The Kingdom of God in the Teaching of Jesus* (Philadelphia: Westminster, 1963), 201–6; Ladd, *Presence*

In this era the kingdom involves the inaugural inbreaking of God's power, presence, and rule among a people whom God has claimed as his own and who claim by faith to have allegiance to God.

At the center of this faith and at the core of this promise stands God's work in and through his unique sent representative, Jesus, and the one this representative has sent, the Holy Spirit, to mark out those of faith as God's people. Through Jesus and the Spirit, God is forming these disciples into a community that looks forward one day to the total inbreaking of God's authority expressed throughout the world. Those who are his have acknowledged their need for God and his provision by faith alone. As a result, they have entered into an enduring relationship with God. That relationship entails God's claim on the life of the disciple.

Thus, in a sense, all aspects of Jesus's teaching about discipleship involve teaching about the kingdom and ethics. In sum, what Jesus presents is the idea that the inbreaking of God's rule into one's life demands a total response to that rule. However, by means of God's grace as directed by God's Spirit, disciples are enabled to move into that demand and grow in their experience of it. Relationship to that rule is to be more important than family, possessions, vocation, even life itself. Perhaps the better way to say this is that existence with God infuses all these other relationships with a dimension they otherwise might lack, resulting in a reprioritization of these core elements of life. So Jesus alludes to the fact that his family is made up of those who do God's will; he says one must hate family for his sake. Family is oriented to the kingdom. Jesus teaches that possessions are to be given to the poor. What we own is to be used in service to others. Vocation is to be undertaken in a way that loves and serves. A job is about more than earning money or making a living. Jesus asserts the need to bear one's cross. One should recognize that the world may not welcome such a restructuring of life along lines that push for service over self-concern. In sum, Jesus is pointing out that no demand on a person's soul is greater than the one made by God in

---

of the Future, 278–304; Scot McKnight, *A New Vision for Israel: The Teachings of Jesus in National Context* (Grand Rapids: Eerdmans, 1999), 156–237; Richard Burridge, *Imitating Jesus: An Inclusive Approach to New Testament Ethics* (Grand Rapids: Eerdmans, 2007).

the context of his kingdom program. The greatness of the kingdom creates the totality of its call for faithfulness.

To develop this area, I examine four themes that ultimately are also tied to the kingdom hope: faith/repentance;[12] following Jesus at all costs by responding from within; imitation in the context of reconciliation, love, and service; and reward. I introduce the themes here and develop some of them later, in the section on the new community (chap. 6 below). Any treatment of kingdom that does not move into this area has failed to appreciate a major practical goal of the kingdom program as the Jesus of Scripture presents it. The kingdom Jesus preached was designed to impact life.

1. The theme of faith/repentance is seen in two key elements. First, there is the preparation that John the Baptist brought by declaring that the kingdom draws near. This preparation highlighted preaching a baptism of repentance, a baptism that included a concrete call for turning expressed in practice toward others (Luke 3:10–14). This idea will be taken up more fully when we get to the theme of imitation, but its groundwork was laid in John's initial, preparatory declaration as an Elijah-like figure. His work involved a call to reconciliation in which people were implored to turn back to God. John's baptism involved participation in a one-time washing that said, "I am ready for God's program to come." Included within this turning was a change that would bring children back to their parents and the disobedient back to the wise (Luke 1:16–17). Reconciliation with God means reconciliation with others. Turning back to God showed itself in

12. I join these two terms into one because they work as equally adequate summary terms for the appropriate response to the message. However, they are not exact synonyms. Repentance looks at that response from the angle of where one starts (there is a change of direction), while faith highlights where one ends up (trusting God). Repentance involves turning: the Hebrew verb behind the idea is *šûb*, which means to turn (Mark 4:12 uses Isa. 6:9–10 to show the connection). Such terms ("faith" and "repent") overlap without being exact synonyms, much like a Venn diagram in math. Thus they can serve as equivalents for each other while focusing on distinct aspects of the fundamental response. Baptism and indwelling are similar. Baptism points to washing, while indwelling points to what results from the washing, the entering in of the Spirit. In OT conceptual terms, forgiveness yields cleansing (or washing) so that the Spirit may come in and indwell (Ezek. 36:24–27). God cleanses so that he can enter into a clean space. Careful attention to such lexical relationships adds depth to the text's message. See Bock, *Recovering the Real Lost Gospel*, chap. 2.

how others were now going to be treated. Luke 3:8–14 speaks of the fruit of repentance and in each case looks at how others are treated as the indicator that repentance has taken place.

The second element in Jesus's teaching on repentance and faith says that to enter the kingdom one must be like a child (Matt. 18:2–4). The image evokes humility and dependence. That humility may well include a "humiliation" that involves suffering and sacrifice. In fact, it is humility that defines "greatness" in the kingdom.[13] Humility also describes a core element that is encased within faith. To trust someone else for spiritual well-being is to acknowledge our inability to provide it for ourselves. So faith in God merges with humility and means God must do what I cannot do for myself. In this context, it is clear that it is not the kingdom in the future that is addressed, because the chapter focuses on relationships in the newly formed community (see Matt. 18:17). Such faith in God extends to a recognition that even daily needs are in his hands and that he will care for his own (Matt. 6:11, 25–34; Luke 11:3; 12:22–31).

Faith ultimately is a humble recognition that one needs God and so moves to trust him, relying on his rule and provision. John's Gospel expresses this idea in terms of eternal life and of knowing God and his sent one (John 17:1–3). This knowledge of God takes place in a context in which the world rejects Jesus and the disciples who know him (John 17:4–26). It is in the context of relying on God's provision that the gospel message also moves in a direction that we are most familiar with through the Pauline emphasis on the work of the cross in relationship to sin. However, one should not forget that alongside God's fundamental provision of forgiveness comes an enablement of provision and power through the Spirit that changes one's identity and allows the disciple to live in a way that honors God and reflects the ongoing connection to him as his child. Forgiveness has a goal: to render one clean and guiltless so that the Spirit can indwell a vessel that is declared clean and guide one into the life that pleases God. In fact, Paul's burden in Rom. 1–8 is to make this very point about the

13. This stress on humility probably explains Jesus's focus on reaching out to those on the fringes of society, the poor, and the tax collectors. Here are people who, as seeming "outsiders," more easily understand their need for God. Jesus clearly focused his message toward such people (Luke 4:16–19).

gospel. It is why Paul describes the gospel as being about the "power" of God (Rom. 1:16). God gives an enablement to walk with him as a core part of the gospel that we cannot supply for ourselves. As an orientation and not just a moment of decision, faith trusts God for that ongoing enablement and direction. Such trusting belief responds to what God gives in the Spirit and how God guides and commands as he shows the way to please him in life.

2. Following Jesus at all costs by responding from within oneself raises the issue of how demanding Jesus's call to discipleship was. It was a cost to be fully counted and not entered into lightly or unadvisedly (Luke 14:25–35). Like a marriage commitment, it was to be a priority. The fact that disciples left their nets or tax-collection booths to follow Jesus shows the commitment level (Mark 1:16–20 par.; Luke 5:28). Jesus expresses it as hating or leaving mother and father for his sake or the kingdom's sake (Luke 18:29; Matt. 10:37; 19:29). It means hating mammon (Matt. 6:24; Luke 12:14–21; 16:13). It involves carrying the cross, even daily, even at the risk of life (Matt. 10:38–39; Luke 9:23).

The assumption in all of this is that the way will not be easy nor the road one of powerful triumph. Victory comes through suffering and rejection like that which Jesus himself would experience. Jesus sought to reveal the whole program to the multitudes. He desired that they understand what was involved in the relationship with God that they were entering into. God's rule is not selective; it makes claims on the whole life. So Jesus defines the members of his family as those who do God's will (Mark 3:31–35 par.; 10:29–30 par.). Sons and daughters respond to the Father. They "seek his kingdom" and rest by faith in his care (Luke 12:31), what Matthew's Gospel calls seeking "first his kingdom and his righteousness" (Matt. 6:33). Faith is seen not merely as belief in certain ideas but as trust in a person, opening the door to being responsive to him. For the one who trusts responds to the one being trusted.

Where Mark emphasizes the readiness to serve and suffer by following after Jesus (Mark 10:35–45), Matthew focuses on a practical righteousness that reflects a life of integrity, as the Sermon on the Mount reveals (Matt. 5–7). Luke also has a practical turn, but his emphases focus on the compassionate treatment of enemies (Luke

6:27–36), a concern for the poor (Luke 4:16–18; 7:22–23; 14:12–14), and avoiding the danger of materialism (Luke 8:14; 12:13–34; 16:19–31; 18:18–30; 19:1–10). John's teaching on how disciples might glorify God in faithfulness before a hostile world belongs here (John 14–17).

Following Jesus in this manner also entails a response from within. Mark 7:1–23 shows this clearly when Jesus defines defilement in terms that look at "what is inside" the person. The list highlights the acts that defile as primarily associated with relational categories. Defiling represents damage done to relationships.

The six antitheses of the Sermon on the Mount press the law in this inward direction. It is not just murder but also anger that violates God's righteous standard, nor is it just adultery but also lust (Matt. 5:21–48). This internal feature stands at the heart of kingdom spirituality[14] and is central to what goes into spiritual formation. That formation is spiritual because God calls and goes to work on the inner person, on our spirit, through the Holy Spirit. This also is not mere triumphalism, as Paul makes clear, since we groan for the completion of redemption in the salvation to come (Rom. 8). We know that God is at work in us until he returns or our life comes to an end. None of us have arrived in this life. In the meantime, the call is to be faithful and walk by the Spirit.

3. Following Jesus naturally leads to the theme of imitation. The child is to be like the Father. One dimension of this concept is the theme of reconciliation. We identified reconciliation as a defining quality of a "prepared" people for God. In Luke 1:16–17, the work of John in calling people to repent brings fathers back to children and the righteous back to the unrighteous. In responding to the Baptist, people were accepting the call of God to be a reflection of him and his holiness. A creation disturbed by broken relationships moves toward restoration through turning back to God and to each other. Love for God expresses itself in love for one's neighbor, laying the groundwork for the great commandment.

What God would provide through the Messiah, as John noted, would be a greater baptism by the Spirit, the great provision of the

14. For a fine discussion of this internal-spiritual theme in light of the Sermon on the Mount, see Dallas Willard, *The Divine Conspiracy: Rediscovering Our Hidden Life in God* (San Francisco: HarperSanFrancisco, 1998).

new era that was the product of forgiveness of sins. By his grace the Spirit enables the transformation that God's kingdom calls for from those who trust God. That faith trusts God to provide for spiritual well-being and deliverance. Jesus makes the same point in the upper room (John 14–16). Jesus must go so that he can send the Paraclete, the Spirit, to enable them to appreciate what Jesus has taught them. So Jesus issues a call to love and serve that imitates God's own character (Luke 6:27–36). This extends even to loving one's enemies. Jesus holds up his own life as the example to be imitated (Mark 10:41–45; John 13:1–17).

Such a character is revealed in the Beatitudes (Matt. 5:3–13//Luke 6:20–23). In fact, it is character like this that is salt and light in the world, reflecting the call of what the kingdom citizen is to be (Matt. 5:14–16). So the disciple is to show mercy (Luke 10:29–37). This is why Jesus identified the Jew who quoted the two great commandments of loving God and loving one's neighbor as someone "not far from the kingdom" (Mark 12:28–34). It is also why the commandment to "love one another" was the sign that would identify Jesus's disciples (John 13:34–35). A major goal of the kingdom was to produce children in kind, which is why the standard for character is so high and the demand of the kingdom so great (Luke 6:36; Matt. 5:48).

4. The kingdom is not without its rewards. Chief among them is vindication in judgment and unending relationship with God, as represented in the image of the banquet table. The Father sees the sacrifice and honors it. Such is the promise of Jesus to an uncertain Peter, who in the midst of a longer discussion about who can be saved if the rich are not able to enter the kingdom, desperately asks about who then can be saved (Luke 18:18–30, esp. vv. 23–30). Jesus's reply assures Peter and those he represents. Jesus summarizes the reward that accompanies participation in the kingdom, saying, "I tell you the truth, no one who has left house or wife or brothers or parents or children for the sake of the kingdom of God will fail to receive many times as much in this age, and in the age to come eternal life" (Luke 18:29–30 AT). The Markan parallel, which speaks of the gospel and not the kingdom—showing the inherent relationship between the two—adds that in the present age the kingdom seekers receive "houses, brothers, sisters, mothers, children, and fields, and with

them, persecutions" (Mark 10:29–30). Matthew 25:31–45 adds that the Son of Man's return in his glory brings with him the vindication of those who have reached out to him. The reward declared in the Beatitudes also underscores that although there is suffering and sacrifice now, there will be great reward.

Here again an appreciation for what the future brings impacts how we see ourselves in the present. This hope calls us to live in light of what the future will bring. The future beckons us in the present to reflect as light what we are becoming and will be, to provide a sneak preview of what is to be. The meek will inherit the earth, but they also are to illuminate it. With our security resting in God's power, presence, and hope, the rule of God can bring us to be what God made us to be. God redeemed us to reflect his image in the way he originally designed us to function. Salvation is about not just deliverance but also restoration to a life lived as God designed it to be experienced. This is precisely why one of the more important parables about the kingdom pictures God's word about the kingdom as a seed that is planted and takes root in good soil and whose goal is to produce fruitfulness (Matt. 13:1–9, 18–23 par.). Viewed from the human perspective, it is the goal of the kingdom to produce sons and daughters of God who are fruitful for him and faithful to the design of what it means to be a human made in God's image.[15] In the call to imitation is the call to mirror God's character and presence.

The future exercise of responsibility for faithful stewardship is another dimension of reward that is less clearly developed and is of lesser significance in Jesus's preaching than the theme of vindication and eternal reception. Only a few passages hint at this idea. It is suggested by the note of expanded responsibility in the parable of the talents (Matt. 25:14–30) and the idea of having responsibility over cities in Luke 19:17, 19. The rewarded servants are "set over much" for their faithfulness. The images are specific to the construct of the parable, but they seem to indicate something about reward for stewardship. Heaven will not be about idleness but about serving God well and rejoicing in his presence. The reward for the blessed servant

15. In Pauline terms, in the key mission passage of Titus 2:11–14 this is expressed in terms of the work of God's grace (see also Eph. 2:10).

in Luke 12:43–44 points in a similar direction. This theme may also be indicated in the note about whether to entrust more to a steward who is irresponsible (Luke 16:11–12).

The sum of this teaching suggests a period when the kingdom will still be at work in the exercise of its rule, themes that may relate to the idea of an intermediate earthly kingdom (or millennium) before the eternal state comes.

It is time to pull together much of what has been said. So now I review the description of the kingdom, noting especially what other terms intimately connect to it. This section is important because it provides a bridge to the rest of the NT teaching on the kingdom and the effect of Jesus's life and ministry. So in the next subsection, I treat these implications and note some of the key links to the rest of the NT.

Implications of the Kingdom: Messiah, Spirit, Son of Man, Salvation, Gospel, Overcoming Satan, and Sin

One of the difficult things about working with a concept is being confident that it represents a legitimate association with the biblical term. In this section, I suggest other issues that connect to the kingdom of God theme. The effect of this is to expand the texts that relate to the kingdom theme, but the justification for doing so needs attention because some argue that tying the kingdom to the Messiah or to the present era reads things into the text rather than from it.

Some challenge the inclusion of the current work of the Messiah within the scope of kingdom teaching by arguing how infrequently the two ideas are juxtaposed in the Gospels. Other challenges to this association come from those who emphasize a definition of the kingdom in terms of its future coercive rule. However, Luke makes the connection by associating the explicit teaching of John the Baptist, as he proclaims the nearness of the kingdom, to remarks that he makes about recognizing when and on what basis the Christ comes (Luke 3:15–17). To his Jewish audience, this association of messianic work with kingdom work and presence would be entirely natural. Jesus's submission to John's baptism means that he embraced John's basic message and connection. One of the signs of the kingdom, or of the eschaton, would be the superior baptism indicating that the Messiah had come and had brought the new, long-anticipated era. Here John the Baptist, speaking as one who is picking up the prophetic hope, alludes to the promise of the new covenant, which was to bring forgiveness and a work of God from within. Jesus says as much in John 3 to Nicodemus. The imagery reflects the images of purity from Judaism. Only a washed and clean vessel can be a place that God inhabits. So the provision of forgiveness and the washing that is pictured in it cleanses the vessel so that God may enter in. It is in this sense that John "prepares" the people for the Lord's coming.

It is precisely this promise with this conclusion that Peter preaches in the great sermon at Pentecost (Acts 2:14–41). Peter also refers back to this basic event to determine that Gentiles are rightly included in the community by God (Acts 10:34–43; 11:13–18).[16] This baptism marks a definitive sign of the Messiah's work and the presence of eschatological hope. The Spirit came to be seen as the down payment on God's further kingdom work, representing his presence and rule, what Paul simply calls "our inheritance" (Eph. 1:13–14). In this cluster of concepts, one can find the connection not only between Messiah and eschaton but also between salvation and gospel.

Paul's preaching on the Spirit's work as a part of new-covenant realization (2 Cor. 3–4)—along with the emphasis in the book of Hebrews on the forgiveness of sins coming through the promised Messiah (Heb. 1; 8–10)—fits with this idea. These texts point to the inaugural era of promise, which Jesus identified as kingdom. Here is why Paul could describe the gospel as what was promised to come through the Son of David in Scripture (Rom. 1:2–4). It is also why Paul called the gospel the "power of God unto salvation" in Rom. 1:16–17 (KJV) as an introduction to Rom. 1–8. That book presents the exalted Son's work in terms of forgiveness, filial connection, and Spirit enablement. This combination is the essence of the gospel, a reversal of the penalty and power of sin. It is what Paul elsewhere calls a rescue "out of the authority of darkness" and a transfer "into the

16. Note the allusion back to Luke 3:15–17 in Acts 11:16 as indicating the promise realized. This emphasis is clearest in Lukan theology and developed in Luke-Acts, but the roots go back to themes in Jesus's message. This link runs through all of Luke and Acts, as I have explained in Darrell L. Bock, *A Theology of Luke and Acts: God's Promised Program Realized for All Nations* (Grand Rapids, Zondervan, 2012), 149–76.

kingdom of [God's] beloved Son" (Col. 1:13 AT). Paul also talks about the idea of the mystery now revealed that was previously pointed to in the "prophetic writings," a clear reference to the hope of the Hebrew Scriptures (Rom. 16:25–27). Here the work of Jesus as the Christ brings pardon, deliverance, and adoption-citizenship, all royal works of messianic authority.

The kingdom—both in its inception, where rescue takes place, and at its culmination, when victory becomes complete—is part of a great cosmic battle and reversal against sin and Satan. It is this kingdom program over which Christ is currently ruling (1 Cor. 15:25; Rev. 1:5–6). The current kingdom's link to the ultimate realization of the kingdom appears in 1 Cor. 15:26–28, where Paul describes the ultimate giving over of this same kingdom to the Father at the end. Seen in a larger theological context, this victory represents the reversal of the fall's effects and evidence of a cosmic battle introduced in Gen. 3. It is why the imagery of Rev. 21–22 and the new heaven and new earth look back to the garden of Eden and forward to the new Jerusalem. The book of Revelation is about the completion of the kingdom program. In the return, the kingdom of the world has become the kingdom of "our Lord and his Christ" (Rev. 11:15).

This return includes setting up an intermediate kingdom before the new heaven and earth appear, because of the way Rev. 20:1–7 describes this period. In that text a period of a thousand years is mentioned six times in seven verses. This number is not merely a figure for a long period of time but is part of a calendar in a theodicy that says God knows the program and timing involved in his deliverance. This is why the number is repeated almost like a refrain in a hymn. The book of Revelation is part of an apocalyptic genre whose prophecy answers the question of where and how God's justice and victory will come. In the intermediate kingdom the things said about Israel in all of Scripture fit with Israel's future role in a rule existing among the nations within this history. The promise of God from both OT and NT meets full realization here. It is here as well that Jesus's mix of apocalyptic imagery comes to fruition. Some things involve Israel in this history, while others involve a remade world of the new heaven and earth.

However, the NT makes much less of this national role for Israel than the OT does. There are two reasons for this shift of emphasis.

1. Israel's role is assumed as a given, having already been revealed and treated in detail in the Hebrew Scriptures, which the church embraced. Acts 3:19–21 points back to Moses and the prophets for "the rest of the story." So the NT does affirm that the story about the future has details in it from the OT.
2. The more comprehensive NT concern is the eventual total victory that Jesus brings to the whole of humanity and the creation. To a degree, this relativizes the importance of national Israel's role in the plan. This point also helps to explain why the land is less emphasized in the NT. Since a salvation that in the end time encompasses an earth now existing in peace, borders mean less than they do when national sovereignty needs protection. It is the difference between Europe in the midst of World War II and Europe of the European Union, where moving between nations no longer requires a passport check at the border. Where there is peace, there is reconciliation and brotherhood, not hostility. Another reason the land is less of a concern is that Israel is in the land when the NT is written, so there is nothing to be reclaimed when the Gospels and Epistles are penned.

So it makes more hermeneutical sense for the theological unity of Scripture that the NT complements what God already has committed himself to in the OT. Maintaining a role for national Israel within the kingdom program seems to make the most coherent sense of Paul's argument in Rom. 11, where Israel is not a reference to the church but is treated in distinction from the current structure through which blessing is preached. This approach, known as premillennialism, sees a hope for national Israel (as well as for the nations), with Christ functioning as Israel's Messiah in the future kingdom program. Fulfillment is in Christ for all of this, so a Christocentric perspective stands at the hermeneutical center of promise, but so do covenantal commitments made by God and carried out by the fulfillment that comes in Christ. Jesus declares such hope and so as fulfiller guarantees its taking place. This approach also affirms the fundamental unity of Jew and Gentile in Christ. So the hope for Israel is not about a nationalism but ultimately about the reconciliation God brings to the work of redemptive restoration as all who respond in faith share in God's blessing.

This comprehensive approach to promise and realization solves the difficult unity-diversity question that plagues debates about eschatology. There is soteriological unity (all are one in Christ and share in one unified plan), while there is structural distinction in the different dispensations of God's administration (period of Israel ≠ period of the church ≠ period of the consummated kingdom moving to the new heaven and earth). Such an approach is a better synthesis than merging Israel and the church, as much contemporary NT theology does. The result of such a merged reading means that the promises made to national and ethnic Israel do cease to operate for these original recipients of God's covenantal promise of grace. This raises questions about the commitments coming from God's Word and promises. Such a covenantal merger conflicts with God's faithfulness, which Paul wishes to defend in Rom. 9–11. Instead of reading the text with such a merger in mind, the apostle maintains hope that one day all Israel will be saved, in contrast to Israel's current rejection of Jesus. The current blessing of many more Gentiles one day will also contain the blessing of many from Israel also returning to the fold. To use Paul's imagery from Rom. 11, those original branches cut off from the vine will be grafted back in, so all Israel can be saved.[17] What God has started in bringing Jew and Gentile together he will complete one day for both groups.

So, on the future end of the kingdom calendar is the work of the returning Son of Man to be the vindicating "judge of the living and the dead" (Acts 10:42; cf. Matt. 25:31–46). He is the one who welcomes his own into "the kingdom prepared for you," in which is found not only fellowship but also "eternal life" (Matt. 25:34, 46). It is toward

17. This paragraph outlines my view on a major debate in eschatology that has been a part of the evangelical scene for a long time. See the discussion between Craig Blaising (premillennialism), Robert Strimple (amillennialism), and Ken Gentry (postmillennialism) in *Three Views on the Millennium and Beyond*, ed. Darrell L. Bock (Grand Rapids: Zondervan, 1999). For more on this question, see Darrell L. Bock, "Why I Am a Dispensationalist with a Small 'd,'" *Journal of the Evangelical Theological Society* 41 (1998): 383–96.

this great vindicating moment that the kingdom always is aimed, so that the concept always is looking to that bright future that is the kingdom come in full.

The Epistles draw on this cluster of concepts as they make the point that the era of our rule with Christ has not yet come (1 Cor. 4:8). For example, the author of Hebrews states that all things are not yet submitted to the feet of humankind as God had promised in Ps. 8:5–7. Nevertheless, he extols that we do see Jesus through the suffering of his death crowned with glory and honor, looking for the completion of what God has begun (Heb. 2:5–9). It is also why Peter, using the language of Ps. 110:1, argues that Jesus, as a result of that exaltation, already is "at the right hand of God, with angels, authorities, and powers made subject to him" (1 Pet. 3:22 NRSV). So also Paul extols appreciation for the power that raised Jesus to the right hand of God, "above all rule and authority" in this age and in the age to come (Eph. 1:19–23). Who is right? Is there an incompleteness to what Jesus has done, as Hebrews presents? Or is there an already-extant cosmic subjection, as Peter claims? Does Jesus have full authority now, as Paul's prayer in Ephesians claims, or even as Jesus himself claimed as he introduced the Great Commission (Matt. 28:16–20)? As with the other tensions highlighted in this discussion of the kingdom, this is not an either-or choice but a both-and truth. The victory is obtained already, but the full manifestation of that victory is yet to come.[18]

The God of the Kingdom: The Father Who Knows, Seeks, Vindicates, Judges, and Is Uniquely the Father of the Son

There is no doubt that Jesus emphasized God's sovereignty as directing the arrival of the kingdom.[19] He is a God who can be trusted and knows the needs of his people (Matt. 6:25–34; Luke 12:22–32). He knows the time of the end (Mark 13:32). For Luke, God is the

18. A now-famous illustration of "already but not yet" compares the idea to D-Day. The Allies "won" the war with that invasion. After that event, victory was inevitable and a matter of time, but the full victory occurred later, when full peace finally came.

19. For this section, see George Ladd, *A Theology of the New Testament*, rev. ed. (Grand Rapids: Eerdmans, 1974), 79–88.

designer of what "must be" (δεῖ) in the plan of salvation (Luke 4:43; 24:7, 26, 44). The basis of Jesus's suffering and that of the disciples is that the Father knows what is ahead and will provide and protect in the midst of the experience. Jesus's prayer at Gethsemane resolves itself on this point, as does his teaching in the Olivet Discourse about how disciples can endure persecution. So God is a God who knows, acts, and directs.

But God's great power does not make him distant. Jesus's teaching that God is "Father" (Matt. 6:9; Luke 11:2) makes a relational connection an emphasis in his teaching that was mostly distinct from where Jewish emphases on sovereignty described him. Jesus's use of this form of address for God appears in all the Gospel strata.[20] Jesus used this form especially in his prayers (Mark 14:36; Matt. 6:9//Luke 11:2; Matt. 11:25–26//Luke 10:21; Luke 23:34, 46; John 17:1, 5). This way of addressing God does not appear in the OT. In Judaism, God often is addressed with his name Yahweh or in light of his promise as the God of Abraham, Isaac, and Jacob, as in benediction 1 of the Jewish community prayer known as the Shemoneh Esreh. It is rare as an address in intertestamental Judaism as well (Sir. 23:1, 4; 3 Macc. 6:3, 8; Wis. 14:3). Yet Jesus taught his disciples to appreciate the fact that there is only one who is Father to them (Matt. 23:9). The familial and relational tie this imagery suggests points to the intimacy of being in covenant relationship with God. It also serves to argue that the community of God's people should see themselves as family.

Even more significant is Jesus's address to God as Father in Mark 14:36 or more pointedly "my Father" in Matt. 26:39, 42. Here, in the tensest moment of his life, as he faces death, Jesus rests in God's tender care, submitting as Son to the sovereign Father. It is in "my Father's kingdom" that Jesus looks forward to the day of full realization (Matt. 26:29). Here is a point of connection between kingdom, God, and Son.

Also to be noted is how these texts present Jesus as the obedient son working faithfully through his trust in God. This will become a

20. Joachim Jeremias, *New Testament Theology*, trans. J. Bowden (London: SCM, 1971), 1:62. In Mark: 14:36. In Matthew and Luke teaching material: Matt. 6:9//Luke 11:2; Matt. 11:25//Luke 10:21a; Matt. 11:26//Luke 10:21b. In Matthew: 25:34; 26:42. In Luke: 23:34, 46. In John: 11:41; 12:27–28; 17:1, 5, 11, 21, 24–25.

point to imitate when one turns to the theme of discipleship. When we see God as Father, we are called to have familial faithfulness to him.

The idea of positional sonship is paralleled earlier in Jesus's ministry in an intimacy affirmed even at Jesus's baptism with the divine voice's address of "my beloved Son" and in the recognition that the relationship between Father and Son is unique (Matt. 11:27; Luke 10:21; John 5:17–20). Appreciating Jesus's unique relationship to the Father forms a bridge to a full understanding of who Jesus is ("my" Father texts: Matt. 7:21; 10:32–33; 11:27; 12:50; 15:13; 16:17; 18:10, 14, 19, 35; 20:23; 25:34; 26:29, 39, 42, 53; Luke 2:49; 10:22; 22:29; 24:49; plus 22 occurrences in John). These texts are found in unique Matthean material, unique Lukan material, and some Matthean-Lukan texts (= Q). The expression is multiply attested. When a theme shows up across the many strands of Gospel tradition, we are in touch with a major note of Jesus's teaching.

God also is a God who invites and seeks. This is especially brought out in the parables of Luke 15 and in the nature of Jesus's mission to and befriending of tax collectors and sinners. Jesus sees himself called by God to be a physician to the sick (Mark 2:15–17; Matt. 9:9–13//Luke 5:27–32). The extent of Jesus's initiative to seek the sinner reveals God's heart in bringing the kingdom. This intimate note was unprecedented within Judaism in its emphasis on God's initiative toward sinners.

The God who invites and fellowships is portrayed above all in the image of the banquet table, where many are present, including some who might not be expected to be there (Matt. 22:1–14//Luke 14:15–24; cf. Matt. 8:11). Such associations brought a charge against Jesus that he was a friend of the wrong type of people (Luke 15:1; Matt. 11:19// Luke 7:34). God's grace extends to those outside the community and is a model for how true "children of God" should act (Matt. 5:45; Luke 6:35–36). God takes the initiative to draw such people to himself, and so should God's people as they carry out God's mission.

However, that God is gracious does not prevent him from exercising his vindicating judgment. God does not have a blind eye when it comes to sin and unrighteousness. Taking up where John the Baptist left off (Matt. 3:12; Luke 3:7–9), Jesus also affirmed a reckoning with God, a reckoning in which the "Son of Man" would have a key role

(Matt. 10:32–33; 11:22–24; 18:6; 23:33; 25:34, 41; Mark 3:29; Luke 10:14–15; 12:4–12). Even Israel and its capital would not be spared for its unfaithfulness in a judgment that was a sign of the coming of the end (Matt. 23:37–39; 24:15; Mark 13:14; Luke 13:34–35; 19:41–44; 21:20–24; 23:27–31). The clearest text is the parable of the judgment of the sheep and the goats (Matt. 25:31–46). In the end, the God of the kingdom will sort out who belongs there from among the nations on the basis of their response to him as seen in their care of those who are his (a view like what Gen. 12:3 says of the response to Abraham's seed). The coming of the kingdom is an opportunity to be blessed and to experience God's grace, but it also means that a separation is coming one day to which all will be accountable (Matt. 13:24–30, 36–43). Of all the Gospels, Matthew makes an emphasis of this point.

Summary on the Kingdom

The treatment of Jesus's teaching on the kingdom shows how comprehensive a concept it is for him. The theme laid the groundwork for much of what we see in the rest of the NT about blessing among God's people. Here was God's promise coming to fruition now in reforming and gathering the righteous to God through the announcement, call, and work of God's unique representative. Jesus was the promised one, bearing the promise and Spirit of God's presence in response to a turning to embrace a commitment of faith. What Jesus announced and started in almost hidden fashion, he would complete one day. By Jesus's return, God's rule would decisively enter this history in judgment and prepare the way for a new world. In the meantime, those who allied themselves with Jesus are called to a life of integrity and service as by faith they embrace the hope that Jesus offered, draw on the Spirit he provides, and await the promise's completion.

One final note needs reaffirming about Jesus's kingdom teaching. The discussion of Jesus's teaching on the kingdom has been plagued by an either-or posing of various problems associated with his teaching in the Gospel tradition. Did Jesus declare an apocalyptic or prophetic hope of the kingdom? Did he teach a dynamic presence or discuss a realm of rule? Did his teaching on the kingdom declare its presence already or only its coming in the future? As a rule, this survey has shown that each way of posing the question risks missing a dimension of Jesus's teaching by forcing a choice. Although one element may receive more emphasis than another in each of these contrasts and in particular texts, Jesus's teaching reflects a depth that encompasses all of these elements. These either-or questions are actually both-and themes, with Jesus alternating what he is emphasizing based on the context in view.

In Jesus's teaching there is a focus not only on what Jesus preached about the kingdom of God but also on who the proclaimer of the kingdom is. How did Jesus show who he is? What we shall see is that he did it less by making claims than by acting in ways that revealed who he is.

4

Jesus's Titles: Who Is Jesus?

Appreciating How Jesus's Actions Explain His Claims and His Titles

In modern studies of Jesus, it is much debated how Jesus saw himself. Categories such as a Cynic-like philosopher, charismatic leader, prophet, sage, or messiah are all paraded as the possibilities. The debate is a reflection of how skeptically many view the portraits in the Gospel accounts.[1] The Gospels reflect these categories in part, but none of them adequately summarizes who Jesus is. To appreciate how these texts portray Jesus, we need to survey the range of titles and actions associated with Jesus and what they affirm about him.

1. In thinking of discussions of the historical Jesus that closed out the twentieth century, we see that the spectrum of options is rather full: from the Cynic-like philosopher of John Dominic Crossan, to Hartmut Stegemann's charismatic leader, Ben Witherington's sage, the prophetic reforming figure of E. P. Sanders, Dale Allison's millenarian prophet, the probably messianic figure of John Meier, and N. T. Wright's messianic reformer. For Wright, Jesus has a central role in God's program in fulfillment of God's promise to return to Zion, save Israel, and reach the world in line with covenant promise. For this range of views and the discussion that informs it, see Mark Allan Powell, *Jesus as a Figure in History: How Modern Historians View the Man from Galilee*, 2nd ed. (Louisville: Westminster John Knox, 2013).

That is the goal of the next two chapters. Our survey of this question seeks to summarize the scriptural data. We take titles first, then actions, hoping to show how the actions helped to define and explain the titles applied to Jesus. We start with titles because that is where the scholarly discussion typically starts, but we will argue that this order is not the best way to appreciate how Jesus came to be understood.

Except for the Gospel of John, the key to assembling a portrait of Jesus is not found primarily in the ways Jesus refers to himself. It is not through claims or claiming titles that Jesus revealed the place he has in God's kingdom program. Rather, the key is found in what he does and in what those actions both individually and as a group represent. So I divide the next two chapters into a survey of titles and then actions. The key to the portrait primarily surfaces through what Jesus does and what he says about what he does rather than in self-confession or his use of titles. The one title that is an exception to this emphasis is "Son of Man," Jesus's favorite way to describe himself. The survey of titles will show how Jesus was perceived as people tried to figure out who he was.

People drawn to Jesus were raising a key question: "What is God doing through him?" They were working out who Jesus is from the earth up. So we need to keep two questions before us that are somewhat distinct: (1) What was Jesus doing and saying? (2) How were people perceiving what Jesus was doing and saying? These will not always align with each other: sometimes it took time for Jesus's followers and disciples to grasp what he was saying. Nothing shows this tension and difference more vividly than how the disciples struggled to grasp how it could be that a program involving deliverance would come through a figure who suffered even to the point of death.

The presentation of Jesus from the earth up produces responses that wrestle to grasp the identity of Jesus through what he taught and did. Although allegiance to Jesus is present, exactly what he was saying was not always appreciated; it took time and repetition for understanding to set in. In a few spots in John's Gospel, we are told this explicitly. The disciples did not grasp the importance or connection of what was taking place until after the resurrection (John 2:22; 12:16). Some grasping of what Jesus meant or the significance of what he did took place "on further review" or through reflection.

Titles

Rabbi-Teacher

The term "Rabbi" was not a self-designation of Jesus but a way that others who respected his teaching addressed him. Mark uses it in 9:5; 10:51; 11:21; 14:45. John has it in 1:38, 49; 3:2, 26; 4:31; 6:25; 9:2; 11:8; 20:16. In Matthew, only Judas in the midst of his act of betrayal calls Jesus "Rabbi" (Matt. 26:25, 49). In place of rabbi, Luke opts for the term "Teacher" four times (7:40; 11:45; 12:13; 19:39), probably in deference to his non-Jewish audience. Luke never has Jesus's disciples call him this; only others who observe Jesus use this title. Luke prefers the term "Master" from those who follow Jesus (5:5; 8:24 [2×], 45; 9:33, 49; 17:13). Mark also uses the alternative title "Teacher" ten times in the form of an address, with everyone from opponents to disciples addressing Jesus this way (Mark 4:38; 9:17, 38; 10:17, 20, 35; 12:14, 19, 32; 13:1). John also has this alternative coming from both believers and observers (1:38; 3:2; 8:4; 11:28; 13:13–14, referring also to "Lord"; 20:16).

Addressing Jesus as Teacher or Rabbi shows how important teaching was to his ministry. Yet in Luke the disciples' preferred expression, "Master," makes clear that Jesus represented an authority that made the Teacher description only one aspect of his identity. The observation that Jesus taught with an unusual authority also points in this direction, especially when that teaching is tied to acts such as exorcism (Mark 1:27 [tied to exorcism]; Matt. 7:29 [not as one of the scribes]). The personal authority embedded in Jesus's teaching is clearly expressed in the image of the man who builds his house either on the sand or on the rock: it is *Jesus's* teaching that the wise person responds to and the fool ignores with devastating consequences (Matt. 7:24–27//Luke 6:46–49).

A theme also tied to Jesus's teaching is the authority with which he taught: Mark 1:27 (//Luke 4:36); Mark 6:2 (//Matt. 13:54); Matt. 8:9//Luke 7:8; Mark 11:28 (//Matt. 21:23//Luke 20:2). Dunn notes why this emphasis on authority is surprising. Jesus lacked formal training.[2] He did not appeal to past tradition, as was common in

2. J. D. G. Dunn, *Jesus Remembered* (Grand Rapids: Eerdmans, 2003), 698–702.

Jewish teaching. Jesus did not focus on exposition of the Torah. He introduced some of his teaching with terms like "amen" ("truly") or "but I say to you." All of this suggests a teacher of a completely distinct class than those who normally taught.

Prophet

The idea that Jesus was a prophet apparently was the most common way for the general populace to view him (Matt. 16:14; 21:11; Mark 8:28; Luke 7:16; 9:19; 24:19). The combination of his teaching and public activity made them think of Jesus as more than a rabbi or mere teacher. Whether he was compared to Elijah (Mark 6:15//Luke 9:8), to the return of John the Baptist, or to a prophet in general, there existed the perception that God was involved in his message.

In Luke, Jesus does not discourage this association. When Jesus gives a synagogue message that Luke details uniquely (Luke 4:16–30), Jesus speaks of himself in these terms. He compares himself to a "prophet . . . without honor" in his hometown (Mark 6:4) and mentions Elijah and Elisha. That text also mixes in potential messianic imagery in the invocation of the Servant portrait from Isa. 61:1–2 and its tie to Jesus's earlier anointing at the baptism. So sometimes when Jesus mentions the prophet image, he also places it alongside eschatological teaching. The image of an eschatological prophet was common in Judaism (Mal. 4:5–6; Sir. 48:9–10; 1QS 9.11). The Gospels depict Jesus as a prophet rejected, like the prophets of old, a theme underscored by Luke 13:31–33, where Jesus says that a prophet "cannot . . . perish away from Jerusalem."[3]

Jesus "came" with a mission tied to teaching and calling. So texts like Mark 2:17 (//Matt. 9:13//Luke 5:32), Matt. 10:34 (//Luke 12:49), and Mark 10:45 (//Matt. 20:28) fit here. Jesus calls sinners: he came to bring a sword that distinguishes, to serve, and to be a ransom for many.

Much of Jesus's activity, especially as he travels to Jerusalem in Luke, has this prophetic feel. However, it is more in the sense of a leader-prophet like Moses, a category that borders on royal-political emphases.[4] Hints of this leader-prophet emphasis exist when Jesus

3. Ibid., 661–62, defending the authenticity of this saying.

4. David Moessner, *Lord of the Banquet: The Literary and Theological Significance of the Lukan Travel Narrative* (Minneapolis: Fortress, 1989); Scot McKnight, "Jesus

declares John to be the last of the great prophets (Luke 7:26; 16:16; Matt. 11:11–15) and then speaks of the coming of the kingdom. Jesus as a prophet announces and leads into the kingdom era, but in leading the way to the new era, he shows himself to be far more than a prophet. He is greater than Jonah the prophet or Solomon the royal sage (Matt. 12:40–42; Luke 11:29–32). John pointed to the eschaton; Jesus brings its inauguration. Jesus not only preaches the will and way of God; he also brings it. So in the end, "prophet" is not the most comprehensive category to apply to Jesus (Luke 24:19–27; John 6:30–33, 49–51). Yet as a leader-prophet, Jesus shows himself to be a hub eschatological figure, even suggesting messianic dimensions. As the parable of the wicked tenants shows, Jesus comes as Son in contrast to servants who depict the prophets (Mark 12:1–12//Matt. 21:33–46//Luke 20:9–19). So looking to the various ways Jesus is shown to be "Son" adds to the portrait.

Son of David

The infancy material of both Matthew and Luke makes a major point of Jesus's association to David and his messianic position. However, these are narrative remarks or observation by figures around Jesus about him. In this section we focus on Jesus's own teaching and the events of his ministry. Did Jesus share this regal emphasis that the infancy material raises? This heading includes not only texts tied to the name "Son of David" but also the use of the royal psalms with reference to Jesus. As such, this category takes on a significant place in teaching about Jesus and overlaps with the reference to the Messiah in the next subunit. It is here that the heavenly voice at Jesus's baptism marks him out as "Son," using Ps. 2, one of the great royal psalms of promise and regal affirmation. That event serves as the entrance into who Jesus is, the heavenly introduction of him as he launches into ministry. When Jesus is marked out by heaven, it is as regal son that he comes onstage to do his work.

Interestingly, it is especially people in Jesus's audiences, who no doubt long for God's deliverance, who use this title for him. So a blind

---

and Prophetic Actions," *Bulletin for Biblical Research* 10 (2000): 197–232, contains a full taxonomy of OT prophetic actions, those of Moses and those of first-century popular-movement prophets.

man cries out for the "Son of David" to give him sight (Mark 10:46–52//Matt. 20:29–34//Luke 18:35–43). This linkage of Jesus's kingship and healing as Son of David may reach back to traditions about Solomon as exorcist and healer (Josephus, *Ant.* 8.2.5 §§45–46; Wis. 7:17–22, presented as Solomon speaking; about David himself in Pseudo-Philo, *Biblical Antiquities* 60.1–3). The title or image is raised in the voices of the disciple-pilgrims who enter Jerusalem (Mark 11:10, "kingdom of our father David"; Matt. 21:9, 15, "Son of David"; Luke 19:38 refers only to "the king"). Matthew highlights the "Son of David" title in describing Jesus (1:1; 9:27; 12:23; 15:22; 21:9, 15). Jesus does not stop such affirmations, an important point in wrestling with the question whether Jesus sought to be appreciated as a messianic figure.

The key text, however, is Mark 12:35–37a (//Matt. 22:41–46//Luke 20:41–44). Here Jesus raises a question about the significance of the name "Son of David" and ties it to a discussion of David's addressing this one as "Lord," through appeal to Ps. 110:1. The passage's point again shows how "Son of David," although a messianic title to be accepted, is not as important as the recognition that this one is acknowledged by his father David as "Lord." Jesus poses the dilemma of how, in a patriarchal society, a son can possess such authority over a father. The riddle is left unanswered except to suggest that "Son of David" is a title of lesser significance than the lordship authority even an ancestor grants to the king to come. Once again an acknowledged description is accepted but also is shown to be ultimately inadequate.

Messiah, Christ, King of the Jews

The title "Christ" is one that all the Gospels use within their narratives (Matt. 1:16; 2:4; 11:2; Mark 1:1; Luke 2:11, 26; 4:41; 23:2; 24:26, 46; John 1:17; 1:41; 3:28; 4:29; 7:26–42; 10:24; 11:27; 12:34; 17:3; 20:31). The titulus on the cross marking Jesus out as "King of the Jews" moves in this direction as well (Mark 15:26//Matt. 27:37//Luke 23:38//John 19:19; Mark 15:32).[5] This narrative use is distinct, however, from considerations of Jesus's use or his reaction to others who raise the title.

5. The nature of Jewish messianic expectation is discussed in chap. 4 of Darrell L. Bock, *Studying the Historical Jesus* (Grand Rapids: Baker Academic, 2002).

Seven scenes here are key. First is Peter's confession at Caesarea Philippi, where the Synoptics share the use of this title as the christological core of the key disciple's confession. Jesus accepts this utterance, especially as it stands in contrast to the populace's view of him as being only a prophet. However, Jesus also redefines the confession quickly in terms of his approaching suffering, so that the term is not merely one of glory but also takes on overtones of the Servant who suffers (Matt. 16:13–23//Mark 8:27–33//Luke 9:18–22).[6] The need to explain this role as Messiah leads Jesus here and in several other places to restrict making a point of the title publicly (Mark 1:25// Luke 4:35; Mark 1:34//Luke 4:41; Mark 3:12//Matt. 12:16; Mark 1:44//Matt. 8:4//Luke 5:14; unique to Mark: 8:30; 9:9 [the parallel in Luke 9:36 notes only that the disciples said nothing but does not explain why]).

This restriction has become known as "the messianic secret." The disciples confess Jesus as Christ, but he prohibits them from making this confession public. The reasons for this limitation appear twofold. (1) The various views of who Messiah is to be in Second Temple Judaism meant that the expectation generated by this title would be counterproductive for Jesus. Since one might expect a transcendent figure (*1 En.* 37–71), a political deliverer (*Pss. Sol.* 17–18), or one political messiah alongside a priestly messiah (some texts at Qumran, e.g., 1QS 9.11), the title would have required too much qualification for public proclamation. (2) Jesus's calling also included a sense of suffering, so using a term that simply meant power and victory would be confusing. Until it became clear to the disciples what "Messiah" meant for Jesus, the term was best left unused.

Jesus's hesitation to publicly confess himself as Messiah and his restricting the disciples from doing so cause Dunn to argue that Jesus did not see himself as messianic. Dunn answers the question whether Jesus saw himself as Messiah with a "qualified no."[7] We prefer to

6. On the significance of the confession at Caesarea Philippi, what is said after it is developed in detail, along with discussion of authenticity issues, see Michael Wilkins, "Peter's Declaration concerning Jesus' Identity in Caesarea Philippi," in *Key Events in the Life of the Historical Jesus: A Collaborative Exploration of Context and Coherence*, ed. Darrell L. Bock and Robert L. Webb (Tübingen: Mohr Siebeck, 2009), 293–381.

7. Dunn, *Jesus Remembered*, 652. He walks through his view in 647–704.

answer this question with a "qualified yes." Jesus saw himself as Messiah, but not in the sense Jews generally had expected. The suffering-to-exaltation sequence is key to this qualification.

Second is the Pharisees' attempt to get Jesus to rebuke his disciples for their confessing Jesus as king, another detail unique to Luke (19:39–40). Here Jesus refuses to stop them and says that if they did not speak, creation would "cry out." Jesus's willingness to go public in the climactic scenes of his last week in Jerusalem signals a change of strategy at this final decisive point in his ministry.

Third is the scene at Jesus's examination before the Jewish leadership (Matt. 26:57–68//Mark 14:53–65//Luke 22:66–71). Here the question about whether Jesus is the Christ eventually evokes a positive though qualified response from Jesus in terms of exaltation, appealing to the Son of Man image and the picture of one at God's right hand from Ps. 110:1, another royal psalm. This affirmation not only of Jesus's messianic authority but also of his exaltation to authority at the side of God, implying his shared equality, is judged to be blasphemous. Thus the theologians acknowledge the import of Jesus's claim of a messianic role by the end of his ministry, even as they reject it. They sense the comprehensive way Jesus is claiming to be the Messiah and react against it.[8]

Fourth is the emphasis that emerges at the examination by Pilate, whether one works with the Synoptics or John (Matt. 27:11–14//Mark 15:2–5//Luke 23:2–5; John 18:29–38). These accounts all focus on the discussion that Jesus was "King of the Jews," a point reinforced by the charge on the placard attached to the cross. The discussion makes sense, since Pilate would not be interested in a religious dispute over Jesus's claims. However, if Jesus's claims had political overtones, then as governor he would need to protect the interests of Caesar. When Jesus is crucified, he is legally seen by Pilate to be guilty of sedition.[9] Jesus accepts the title, although with an affirmation suggesting that he

8. For a detailed discussion of what this scene means and a detailed defense of its historical authenticity, see Darrell L. Bock, "Blasphemy and the Jewish Examination of Jesus," in Bock and Webb, *Key Events in the Life of the Historical Jesus*, 589–667.

9. For a detailed discussion of the historical credibility of this scene and the significance of its meaning, see Robert L. Webb, "The Roman Examination and Crucifixion of Jesus," in Bock and Webb, *Key Events in the Life of the Historical Jesus*, 669–773.

views it differently from Pilate (Mark 15:2//Matt. 27:11//Luke 23:3). In this context, the confession is virtually messianic.

As we turn to examples from John, Jesus is more direct. Fifth is the discussion in John 4, where Jesus reveals himself as the Messiah to the Samaritan woman (John 4:25–26). Sixth is the discussion with the blind man and his family in John 9, where the confession of Jesus as the Christ has yielded a reaction from officials to expel those who make the confession (John 9:22). Seventh is Martha's confession of Jesus to be "the Christ, the Son of God, . . . who is coming into the world" (John 11:27). In each of these examples, the revelation about Jesus's identity is private rather than public. Martha responds by confessing Jesus as the Christ when Jesus raises the issue of his authority over resurrection. All the Johannine texts are ways of affirming Jesus as the unique and promised sent one of God; yet they also somewhat reflect Jesus's reluctance to make a broadly public point of the title. The way in which Jesus might be perceived impacted how he talked about himself. He preferred to display his role through his actions versus proclaiming who he is.

Other Titles: Servant, Holy One, Shepherd

These remaining titles can be treated more briefly because their explicit use is not that common. The title "Servant" comes only in narrative remarks (Matt. 12:18 in its use of Isa. 42:1–4). However, aspects of the description of the Servant appear as allusions to the Isaianic Servant Songs. The voice at the baptism calls Jesus "the Beloved" in allusion to Isa. 42:1 (Matt. 3:17//Mark 1:11//Luke 3:22), a remark repeated at the transfiguration (Mark 9:7//Matt. 17:5//Luke 9:35). The death of Jesus is associated with sacrifice in language that looks at Isa. 53 in the Last Supper, in all likelihood in the ransom saying (Matt. 20:28//Mark 10:45), and in Jesus being reckoned among criminals at his death (Luke 22:37). Again, the title is not one that Jesus himself confesses but is tied to actions that raise the imagery.[10]

10. On the importance of this imagery, see William H. Bellinger and William R. Farmer, eds., *Jesus and the Suffering Servant: Isaiah 53 and Christian Origins* (Harrisburg, PA: Trinity, 1998), esp. the essay by Otto Betz, "Jesus and Isaiah 53," 70–87.

Many connect the idea of Jesus needing to suffer as the Christ with this image of the Servant who suffers.

The Johannine equivalent of Caesarea Philippi is Peter's confession at the end of John 6 that Jesus is "the Holy One of God." Peter goes on to declare that Jesus has the words of eternal life (John 6:68–69). This is another way to say that he is the promised one who brings the life of deliverance. Mark and Luke also use this title in the confession by demons (Mark 1:24; Luke 4:34). Again, the description is found on the lips of one trying to affirm who Jesus is, even reflecting the awareness of cosmic enemies.

A key image of a leader-king of the people is "the Shepherd." One can think of 2 Sam. 7:8, where the hope of Davidic kingship is introduced. One can also reflect on the role of leader of the people in the rebuke of Ezek. 34. The rebuke of leaders in that passage leads to the declaration that God will shepherd his people one day and give them a royal shepherd of righteousness (Ezek. 34:11–12, 23–24). This image stands behind Matthew's observation on what motivated Jesus: he saw people who were "like sheep without a shepherd" (Matt. 9:36). It also is key to the imagery of John 10, where Jesus refers to himself as the good shepherd. This is a role that Jesus views as central to his call.

Thus, these three titles are other ways to refer to Jesus as the unique one sent by God to deliver and bring the new era of peace. They are equivalents to arguing that Jesus is the promised Christ of the new era of deliverance and hope.

Lord

This title was key in the early church, but it appears less prominently in the Gospels. Often it is merely a vocative of address (like "sir"), a title of respect where the person's exact view of Jesus is unclear (Matt.

Betz argues for the backdrop of Isa. 52:14 and 53:1 in the remarks that Jesus makes when he is anointed by the woman at Bethany in Matt. 26:13 and Mark 14:9, as well as in John 12:32–38 in the idea of the Son of Man being lifted up. The first of these allusions is less than clear. More solid are appeals to Jesus's allusion to Isa. 53 in Mark 10:45 and 14:22–24. Betz defends the authenticity of these sayings while making his case. For details on the meaning, authenticity, and significance of the Last Supper, see I. Howard Marshall, "The Last Supper," in Bock and Webb, *Key Events in the Life of the Historical Jesus*, 481–588.

15:27; 18:21; Mark 7:28; Luke 7:6; 9:59; 11:1; 12:41). It also appears frequently in Luke as a narrative description for Jesus (Luke 7:13, 19; 10:1; 13:15, 23; 17:5; 18:6; 24:3 NKJV). The last example in Luke is important because it and 24:34 show that this title became associated with Jesus's resurrection. It is the Lord who was raised.

In other texts, it is clear that the title points to Jesus's status, but just what it confesses is unclear. So when Peter bows before Jesus to confess himself as a sinful man, the scene suggests Jesus's holiness and association with God as a revealing agent (Luke 5:8). In Matt. 7:21, those who confess Jesus as Lord but fail to do what he commands are rebuked. In Matt. 21:3//Mark 11:3//Luke 19:31, the man supplying the donkey for the entry into Jerusalem is told, "The Lord has need of it." Again, exactly how Jesus is seen is unclear, but his superior stature is evident from the use of this title.

Two Synoptic texts are more important. One is the already-discussed treatment of "Son of David" versus "Lord" in Matt. 22:45//Mark 12:37//Luke 20:44. Here it is clear that Jesus intends "Lord" to be a key title and that it is associated with the exalted imagery of Ps. 110:1, where this figure sits at God's right hand. It is a more important title than Son of David, which looks to a regal status. So it means more than king.

This right-hand imagery became connected with the resurrection-ascension in the early church. The text makes this point through the image of being seated at the right hand: it appears in Jesus's reply as he is examined by the Sanhedrin in Matt. 26:64//Mark 14:62//Luke 22:69. As a result, Jesus's lordship became associated with his position at God's side as a result of God's vindication and exaltation of him through resurrection.[11] He is able to be at God's side and share rule and authority with him. The affirmation raises key questions: Who can sit with God in heaven? What does that mean about who Jesus is? In a Judaism where monotheism reigns, this was a crucial affirmation with vast implications. It helped to define Jesus's status and person as occupying a position with God. It is a key text in thinking about Jesus from the earth up.

11. The background to the teaching of this text is the burden of one of my monographs: Darrell L. Bock, *Blasphemy and Exaltation in Judaism and the Final Examination of Jesus*, WUNT 2/106 (Tübingen: Mohr Siebeck, 1998).

Another key text is Mark 2:28//Matt. 12:8//Luke 6:5, where Jesus is "lord of the Sabbath." Here as well the title points to a comprehensive kind of authority that extends even over the commanded day of rest. It is God who set and defines what takes place on the Sabbath, which distinguished Judaism. Claiming authority over this day also says a great deal. The implications of this kind of act will be developed in the chapter on Jesus's actions (in chap. 5 below).

The title "Lord," though rarely used in the context of Jesus's ministry in the Synoptics, suggests the presence of one with divine authority and one who is close to God. Interestingly, John's Gospel has a similar thrust.

We notice the shift in use of "Lord" between John 1–19 and John 20–21. In three uses in John 1–19 (4:1 [variant reading]; 6:23; 11:2), it is simply a narrative remark from the evangelist. In addition, others address Jesus as "Lord," but in most cases exactly what is meant is not clear (some as "Sir," some as "Lord": John 4:11, 15, 19, 49; 8:11; 9:36, 38 [in connection with confessing Jesus as Son of Man]; 11:3, 12, 21, 27 [tied to confession of Jesus as Christ and Son of God], 32, 34, 39; 12:21; 13:6, 9, 13–14, 37; 14:5, 8, 22).

When we come to John 20–21, things change. Like the use of "Lord" in Luke, John also focuses frequently on "Lord" in discussing the resurrection. It appears fifteen times in two chapters, more than half being descriptions of Jesus, not addresses of respect to him (John 20:2, 13, 18, 20, 25, 28; 21:7 [2×], 12). None is more important than when Thomas cries out, "My Lord and my God!" upon seeing the risen Jesus (20:28). Here the term takes on its full meaning, a sense that it clearly also had in the early church. The recognition of the risen Lord led to reflection on what that meant for his authority and position in relationship to God. When God raised and vindicated Jesus, it confirmed Jesus's message, claims, and the central role he had in executing kingdom blessing. What is amazing is how restrained this usage is within the events of Jesus's life for a tradition that many critics argue is full of later Christology inserted into the Gospel tradition. The restraint may well suggest that the Gospels do not express Christology as anachronistically as some critics argue.

Son of God

The term "Son of God" is full of ambiguity because of its potential royal implications through the imagery of 2 Sam. 7 and the royal psalms, such as Ps. 2. As such, the term serves as one of two good bridge terms, along with "Son of Man."

In the Synoptics, Jesus does not use this full phrase for himself, although he does speak of himself as "Son" in several texts and frequently claims God as his Father (e.g., Matt. 11:25–27//Luke 10:21–22). The title appears nine times in John's Gospel: 1:34 (a confession by John the Baptist); 1:49 (part of a confession by Nathanael in a messianic context); 3:18 (a narrative remark); 5:25 (in a major discourse on the Father-Son relationship); 10:36 (a cause for Jesus being accused of blasphemy); 11:4 (the recipient of glory to come from Lazarus's illness); 11:27 (part of a confession by Martha); 19:7 (a reason for Jewish leaders wanting to kill Jesus); 20:31 (a narrative remark).

More frequently in the Gospels, others designate Jesus as "Son" or "Son of God." This comes in various settings and from a variety of sources. We have already noted its use by the divine voice at Jesus's baptism and transfiguration. Luke 9:35 uniquely interprets this to mean that Jesus is the one who "stands chosen" (AT). "Son of God" also is the major title of focus at the temptations (Matt. 4:1–11//Luke 4:1–13). Demons also confess Jesus as the "Son of God" (Matt. 8:29//Mark 5:7//Luke 8:28 [Mark and Luke speak of the "Son of the Most High God"]; Luke 4:41). The Luke 4:41 text is significant because it applies the title to Jesus, and the evangelist explains that the demons "knew that he was the Christ." This ties the titles together, referring to both a regal connection and a special association and role in relationship to God.

Sometimes the suggestion is made that the title "Son of David" or "Messiah" points to an earthly authority, while "Son of God" is more cosmic and tied to spiritual forces.[12] However, texts such as Luke 4:41 or the healing of the blind man by Jesus as Son of David (Matt. 20:29–34//Mark 10:46–52//Luke 18:35–43) make such a clear

12. This appears to be suggested in remarks by Leonhard Goppelt, *Theology of the New Testament*, ed. Jürgen Roloff, trans. John E. Alsup (Grand Rapids: Eerdmans, 1981), 200.

distinction unlikely. What is more likely is that the title "Messiah," which could be understood in strictly earthly terms, is raised to new levels in its association with sonship in the way Jesus eventually discusses it. Interestingly, the only person to call Jesus "Son of God" in Mark is the centurion at the cross (Mark 15:39), a report that Matthew also includes (Matt. 27:54).[13]

Jesus also uses "Son" as a major self-designation. A key text is Matt. 11:25–27//Luke 10:21–22. Jesus as Son is the unique revealer of God, giving knowledge of the Father for which only he can be the mediating source to others. Such use of the title is saved for the disciples until later in Jesus's ministry. This revelatory depiction of Jesus is like the idea so prominent in John's Gospel, where John calls Jesus the "Word" and also speaks of Jesus's key role in revealing the way of the Father in several texts (John 3:14–36; 5:9–27; 6:40; 8:36; 14:13; 17:1). In fact, John 5 presents the Father and the Son as inseparable in will and action. It is a burden of the Christology of John's Gospel to portray Jesus as the Son inseparable from the Father, as John 10:30 directly says: "I and the Father are one." In contrast to the Synoptics—which save such direct declarations of who he is until the last week of Jesus's ministry and instead use an array of titles—John has Jesus speak of himself explicitly as Son throughout his ministry.

A second key Synoptic text is the imagery involved in the parable of the wicked tenants (Matt. 21:33–41//Mark 12:1–12//Luke 20:9–19). Here it is the leadership's rejection of the Son that is prominent. He is the last and the highest figure in a line of servants (prophets) whom the vineyard owner (God) has sent to Israel to look for fruit from the nation. After sending several prophets to Israel, God hopes that Israel will respond positively when he sends the Son. However, even his unique status as Son does not protect him: he is slain. Here, after coming to the capital city and presenting himself as king, Jesus makes his claim of sonship and declares that it will not be accepted. Yet the

13. Mark lacks a reference to Jesus as "Son of God" at Caesarea Philippi that Matthew 16:16 has. Matthew also has the title uniquely as a confession by the disciples at the stilling of the storm (14:33) and in the mocking of Jesus by the passersby, chief priests, and scribes while he hangs on the cross (27:40, 43). The irony of this final scene is that what the leaders mock with derision and doubt, the unfolding events of the narrative demonstrate is true of Jesus.

force of the remarks assumes that he has portrayed himself this way already; otherwise Jesus's allusion to himself as the "beloved son" (Mark and Luke) or "son" (Matthew) does not make sense, nor does the tenants' recognition of this son as "the heir" (all the Synoptics). The parable also portrays vindication coming for the Son. The Father will judge the rejection, a point that Jesus makes by appealing to Ps. 118:22 in a sense that portrays Israel's leadership as enemies of God, for the stone the builders rejected will be exalted by God.[14]

Of course, Jesus's language of God as "my" Father also belongs here. These notes about sonship have multilayered attestation, appearing in Markan, Matthean-Lukan, Matthean (confessions by others only at this level), and Johannine material. This teaching is so deeply embedded that it appears in all the strands of Gospel tradition.

A final key text is the one at Jesus's examination by the Jewish leadership. They ask Jesus whether he is "the Son of the Blessed One" (Mark 14:61 NASB) or "Son of God" (Matt. 26:63, using a more direct reference to God). Luke has this question in his trial scene in a slightly later spot during the interrogation (Luke 22:70). In all three Synoptics, the title appears to be a synonymous appositive to "Christ" in this scene, but that conclusion is not entirely certain. Jesus's reply is qualified in Matthew and Luke but is basically positive. The qualification appears to suggest that Jesus is affirming the title but with a different, more significant meaning than the question from the leadership suggests. In Mark, the reply comes as a simple yes.

Jesus's larger response makes clear how comprehensively he views the title "Son of God." In the context of all three replies comes Jesus's affirmation that he will be at the right hand of God, reinforcing his claim to authority as Son. Luke's summary has the confession as a confirming remark, while Matthew and Mark use it as an introduction to the allusions to Ps. 110:1 (Jesus to be seated at the right hand) and Dan. 7 (Son of Man [all three Synoptics], coming on/with the clouds [Matthew and Mark]). In response to this reply, the leaders declare Jesus to be blaspheming. Sonship at the side of God was something they could not see as possible for Jesus, and thus the claim had to

14. The reversal of the past reading of such psalms, in which Israel was on the blessed side, shows how transforming a decision about Jesus is. A similar reversal shows up in the church's use of Ps. 2 in Acts 4.

be totally rejected. How could a Galilean teacher or even prophet have such an exalted position? In the journey from the earth up, the leaders got stuck here. It is Jesus's claim about his own authority and proximity to God that eventually affirmed their sentence and led to his death. In another irony, the testimony that gets Jesus crucified ultimately comes from his own mouth. In the movement of the Gospel narratives, Jesus is crucified for telling the truth about who he is.

Thus, although "Son" and "Son of God" are used restrictively in the Synoptics, their appearance both in the Synoptics and in John gives rise to much controversy about Jesus. The combination of royal role and divine intimacy wrapped up in the references make "Son of God" an important title, but the most significant title of all for Jesus is the last one we examine, "Son of Man."

Even still today, the titles "Son of God" and "Son of Man" are important for understanding Jesus. The church developed an early understanding of Jesus as sharing in the divine identity as a result of the resurrection-ascension and what that exaltation meant for who Jesus is.[15] The resurrection was the ultimate earth-up explanation for who Jesus is. This event categorically presented Jesus as Son, both Son of God and Son of Man. He was not only "Son" functionally; he really was the only Son, what Paul will later call the firstborn from the dead, preeminent in everything (Col. 1:18). Texts that point to Jesus's absolute authority (Phil. 2:5–11; 1 Cor. 8:6; Rom. 9:5; Heb. 1:5–14; Eph. 1:21–22; Rev. 4–5) or that speak of him as Son in connection with the Father and the Spirit and as possessing all authority (Matt. 28:18–20) acknowledge the rule of the one who is the Son.

In these texts, the implied unique authority in the activity of Jesus's life as Son becomes explicitly affirmed. It is why a careful look at Jesus's actions is so central to appreciating who Jesus is, for actions will speak along with words to make his role clear. The bridge now explicitly crossed through the resurrection and vindication of the Son

15. For a presentation of this emphasis on Jesus sharing the divine identity as part of a very early high Christology in the early church, see Richard Bauckham, *God Crucified: Monotheism and Christology in the New Testament* (Grand Rapids: Eerdmans, 1998). This study has some important corrections to offer on how NT Christology is handled by many in NT studies. The importance of what the resurrection-ascension taught the early church is well balanced in Bauckham's approach, as is his emphasis on how suffering connects to the divine identity.

to sit at God's side shows that John's explicit prologue is a natural conclusion about who Jesus was and is. Not only did the Word become flesh through the incarnation, but also through the resurrection Jesus was seated at the Father's right hand, providing a view of who Jesus is from the earth up. This confirms him as the Word sent to reveal the promise and program of God. This entire sequence is what Paul extols in Phil. 2:5–11: the one who "emptied himself" is now "exalted," so "every knee should bow . . . and every tongue confess that Jesus Christ is Lord, to the glory of God the Father." This Philippians text's appeal to the language of Isa. 45:23 is also significant: what the Hebrew Scriptures say of the God of Israel is now being claimed for Jesus. Texts like these show how the events tied to Jesus's career came to be expounded by the early church.

Son of Man

This title represents Jesus's favorite self-designation. In fact, this title is prevalent in a variety of ways. First, it is almost always on the lips of Jesus. Of its 82 appearances in the Gospels, only John 12:34 has it on someone else's lips. Even in that text the use is triggered by Jesus's own earlier use of the title. The term appears 30 times in Matthew, 14 times in Mark, 25 times in Luke, and 13 times in John. Apparently 51 different sayings are counted in this number,[16] with 14 of them rooted in Mark, 10 involving Matthean-Lukan teaching material, 8 peculiar to Matthew, 7 peculiar to Luke, and 13 found in John.[17] Matthew has several texts on his own (10:23; 13:37, 41;

16. I use the term "apparently" because there is debate about which sayings are parallel and which are unique. Here is the list of texts where "Son of Man" appears: Matt. 8:20; 9:6; 10:23; 11:19; 12:8, 32, 40; 13:37, 41; 16:13, 27, 28; 17:9, 12, 22; 19:28; 20:18, 28; 24:27, 30 (2×), 37, 39, 44; 25:31; 26:2, 24 (2×), 45, 64; Mark 2:10, 28; 8:31, 38; 9:9, 12, 31; 10:33, 45; 13:26; 14:21 (2×), 41, 62; Luke 5:24; 6:5, 22; 7:34; 9:22, 26, 44, 58; 11:30; 12:8, 10, 40; 17:22, 24, 26, 30; 18:8, 31; 19:10; 21:27, 36; 22:22, 48, 69; 24:6–7; John 1:51; 3:13, 14; 5:27; 6:27, 53, 62; 8:28; 9:35; 12:23, 34 (2×); 13:31.

17. Joachim Jeremias, *New Testament Theology*, trans. J. Bowden (London: SCM, 1971), 1:260. Jeremias later (1:262–63) reduces the number of authentic sayings by arguing that 37 of the 51 Gospel sayings have parallels in which the term is missing or has "I" in its place. Jeremias argues by using the sequence of Markan priority as key. But even if this is the order of the Gospels, matters are not so simple. Is it not more likely that a Gospel writer would remove or simplify the reference to a title that has fallen out of use than to introduce it into the tradition to give it an archaic

16:28; 24:30, 39; 25:31; 26:2). Luke has several as well (12:8; 17:22; 18:8; 19:10; 21:36; 22:48; 24:6–7). This means that the expression has multiple attestation, showing itself in every Gospel tradition layer. All of John's 13 sayings are unique to his Gospel.

These sayings in the Synoptics have been divided up into three subclasses: sayings about Jesus's present ministry (17 passages), sayings about his suffering (26 passages), and sayings about his role in the end, called apocalyptic sayings (27 passages).[18] Each type is well distributed across each Gospel but with varying emphasis, depending on the Gospel. Matthew has 7 present-ministry sayings, 10 suffering sayings, and 13 apocalyptic sayings. Mark, known for emphasizing Jesus's suffering, has 3 present-ministry sayings, 9 suffering sayings, and 3 apocalyptic sayings. Luke has 7 present-ministry sayings, 7 suffering sayings, and 11 apocalyptic sayings. For John, the subdivisions are different in terms of topic. He has 4 sayings that speak of the coming and going of the Son of Man, 6 sayings that treat crucifixion and exaltation, 1 that names him as judge, and 2 identifying him as salvation bringer.

The key to this title and Jesus's use of it is the imagery from Dan. 7:13–14, where the term is not a title but a description of a figure who rides the clouds and receives authority directly from God in heaven.[19]

---

feel? Furthermore, even if Jeremias is right on some of the examples, turning a direct reference to Jesus into a Son of Man saying or omitting the title still makes the same conceptual point. It still leaves us in touch with Jesus's historical teaching because the ideas were synonymous, given that Jesus was the Son of Man. For these reasons I question his reducing the number of these sayings that go back to Jesus, even if some of the sayings have differences with some of their parallels at this point. All that these differences might show is that in some texts the title "Son of Man" was lacking, but what the concept indicated was not necessarily lacking.

18. Some of these classifications for a particular saying could be debated or in a couple of cases reflect a mixture of categories and thus be counted more than once, leading to the extra number of passages. Working with sayings units, not counting total references, George Ladd (*A Theology of the New Testament*, rev. ed. [Grand Rapids: Eerdmans, 1974], 148–49) has a useful chart of the Synoptic Son of Man sayings. His count: 10 earthly (2 Markan; 3 Q [= material common to Matthew and Luke]; 2 M [= material unique to Matthew]; 3 L [= material unique to Luke]); 9 suffering (3 Markan; 1 Q; 1 Mark and Luke; 4 Mark and Matthew); 18 apocalyptic (3 Markan; 3 Q; 7 M; 5 L). Ladd offers a good discussion of these titles on 143–47, with bibliography. Notice again how each tradition layer is represented across the various kinds of sayings. Multiple attestation applies to the subcategories of this title's usage.

19. For more on this background, see discussions of Mark 13:26//Matt. 24:30//Luke 21:27, and Mark 14:62//Matt. 26:64//Luke 22:69. The bibliography and debate

This OT background to the title does not emerge immediately in Jesus's ministry, but it is connected to remarks made to disciples at the Olivet Discourse and Jesus's reply at his examination by the Jewish leadership. The title is appropriate because of its unique fusion of human and divine elements.

"Son of man" is simply an expression meaning "human being." In contrast to the strange beasts of Dan. 7, this is a figure who is normal, except for the authority he receives. In riding the clouds, this man is doing something otherwise left only to the description of divinity in the OT (Exod. 14:20; 34:5; Num. 10:34; Ps. 104:3; Isa. 19:1). Furthermore, in Aramaic the title was an indirect way to refer to oneself, making it a less harsh way to make a significant claim. Despite its indirectness, the nature of Jesus's consistent use of the term makes clear that he was referring to himself, not to someone else.

All this data shows how widespread this concept was for Jesus, covering the entire realm of his present and future ministry. In his earthly ministry, the Son of Man has authority to forgive sins (Mark 2:10 par.), is Lord of the Sabbath (Mark 2:28 par.), comes eating and drinking in lifestyle (Matt. 11:19//Luke 7:34), and has nowhere to lay his head (Matt. 8:20//Luke 9:58). A word against him can be forgiven (but forgiveness is not available to one who blasphemes the Spirit's testimony about him [Matt. 12:32//Luke 12:10]). He sows good seed (Matt. 13:37), but persecution results from his presence (Luke 6:22). He comes "to seek and to save the lost" (Luke 19:10). When Judas

---

surrounding this title are immense. For two other discussions surveying this background and debate, see Darrell L. Bock, "The Son of Man in Luke 5:24," *Bulletin for Biblical Research* 1 (1991): 109–21; Bock, *Blasphemy and Exaltation in Judaism and the Final Examination of Jesus*, 224–30, which defends the authenticity of the key Son of Man saying at the Jewish examination of Jesus. Some critics try to divide the sayings up into classes and then challenge them, as well as reject the more biblically explicit texts tied to Dan. 7 as being products of the early church, on the premise that they are too developed to be authentic. However, given the evidence that Jesus used the title so extensively, it is hard to believe that he did not root it in a biblical backdrop. For a more detailed defense of Jesus's use of the image, see Bock, "Blasphemy and the Jewish Examination of Jesus," in Bock and Webb, *Key Events in the Life of the Historical Jesus*, 638–56. The rejection of these sayings is hypercritical, taking a divide-and-conquer approach to an expression that is solidly and multiply attested. Key here also are two Jewish texts: *1 En.* 37–71 and *4 Ezra* (= 2 Esd.) 13. They also foresee a figure who exercises judgment in the end, showing that the concept was floating around in or near this period.

betrays Jesus with a kiss, it is the Son of Man whom Jesus says is being betrayed (Luke 22:48).

The suffering Son of Man appears most in passion predictions that Jesus will suffer (Mark 8:31; 9:12, 31 [delivered into human hands]; 10:33 [delivered and condemned]; 14:41 par.; Matt. 12:40//Luke 11:30 [three days in the earth]). Silence about the transfiguration is commanded until the Son of Man is risen (Mark 9:9). The Son of Man came to serve and give his life as a ransom for many, stated in a key text that may well also allude to Isa. 53, thus combining Son of Man and Servant references (Mark 10:45//Matt. 20:28). He is betrayed to sinners (Mark 14:41//Matt. 26:45).

The apocalyptic sayings highlight his coming with the angels, on the clouds, or seated at God's side, all focusing on the heavenly authority that he possesses (Mark 8:38 par.; 13:26 par.; 14:62 par.; Matt. 13:41). He comes at an unknown time (Luke 12:40//Matt. 24:44). Like lightning he comes, illuminating all (Luke 17:24//Matt. 24:27). Like the flood in the days of Noah, he comes suddenly and catastrophically (Luke 17:26//Matt. 24:37). He comes with angels (Matt. 13:41), on a throne (Matt. 19:28), with the heavens shaking (Matt. 24:30), and in glory (Matt. 25:31). It is in these terms that the powerful coming in judgment is described (Matt. 24:39; Luke 17:30). The mission to Israel will not be done before the Son of Man comes (Matt. 10:23). Yet some will not die before they see the Son of Man in glory (a reference to the transfiguration as a precursor to the final glory [Matt. 16:28]). Those who acknowledge Jesus, the Son of Man will acknowledge before the angels (Luke 12:8). But there will be enough delay that the question remains whether the Son of Man will find faith by the time he comes (Luke 18:8). This tension between imminence and delay is a NT theme that is never resolved, since only the Father knows the time of the return. The disciples' prayer is to be that they will prove faithful in the face of all of these things so that they can stand before the Son of Man when he does come (Luke 21:36).

The Johannine statements, even though they take a different form from the Synoptic Son of Man statements, are not as distinct as one might think. The promise that a disciple will see the heavens open up and see the angels ascending and descending on the Son of Man resembles the remarks about Jesus coming in glory or with the angels

(John 1:51). The idea that the Son of Man has authority to judge is inherent in the apocalyptic sayings (John 5:27). The association of the Son of Man with a death that glorifies may well combine ideas expressed in the suffering and apocalyptic sayings of the Synoptics (John 12:23; 13:31). Here is an example of the Gospel of John's emphasis pointing to what Christ does in the present as also related to things normally associated with what he will do in the future. Although the language of being "lifted up" is new, the imagery of the Son of Man suffering is like other Synoptic predictions about his suffering (John 3:14; 8:28). Three of the texts are simply questions about the Son of Man, one asked by Jesus (John 9:35) and another asked by the crowd in association with discussions about the promise of the Christ (John 12:34 [2×]).

Four texts are more distinctive in emphasis, though on closer consideration two of them overlap with Synoptic emphases. The idea of no one having ascended into heaven except the one who descends, the Son of Man, highlights John's focus on Jesus as being sent from heaven (3:15), like the image of the Word become flesh (1:14). Similar to this is the prediction made to grumbling disciples that they should not take offense at Jesus's remarks, for they may see the Son of Man ascending to where he was before (John 6:62). In the next verse, Jesus emphasizes himself as the giver of the Spirit in his teaching. This fits with an earlier remark that Jesus as the Son of Man gives food that endures to eternal life and does not perish (John 6:27). So John highlights the teaching of Jesus as pointing to life and the Spirit. This is similar to the idea of the Son of Man sowing good seed (Matt. 13:37). The most distinctive text is John 6:53, which has Jesus say to the Jews that if they do not eat the Son of Man's flesh and drink his blood, they have no life in themselves. Here Jesus compares himself to a sacrifice consumed at table, even with the hyperbole of consuming his blood. It is a roundabout way of saying that they must identify with his coming suffering and partake of it. Although expressed in a uniquely picturesque manner, the point is not unlike saying the Son of Man suffers as a ransom given for many (Mark 10:45).

The Son of Man sayings summarize Jesus's ministry as the uniquely empowered eschatological agent of God, a human saturated with divine authority. It was self-referential, rooted in Dan. 7:13–14, pointed to vindication and authority, and fit into Jewish expectation.[20] This Son of Man also has a fresh feature tied to its use: he is one who gives himself for the people that he one day will vindicate in glory. A survey of the scope of the usage of the "Son of Man" title helps us to see why Jesus chose it as his favorite way to speak of himself. As Ladd aptly says of the title, "Jesus laid claim to a heavenly dignity and probably to pre-existence itself and claimed to be one who would one day inaugurate the glorious kingdom. But in order to accomplish this, the Son of Man must become the Suffering Servant and submit to death."[21]

God

All of this leads to the very rare use of the simple title "God." In John 1:1 it is found in the narrative remark about Jesus: "the Word was God," or "the Word was divinity" (AT). This saying involves a reflection about Jesus in John's prologue, not an event in Jesus's life or ministry. A similar remark appears in John 1:18 about Jesus as the "only begotten God" (NASB). The one text using the title that is not a narrative remark but appears in the life, ministry, and resurrection of Jesus is the remark of Thomas in John 20:28, when he exclaims, "My Lord and my God!" after seeing the risen Jesus.

Interestingly, what is far more common is the charge that Jesus by his actions is impinging upon God's unique space or prerogatives. So when he forgives the sins of the paralytic in Mark 2:5 (//Matt. 9:2//Luke 5:20) or of the sinful woman in Luke 7:48, the leadership complains that he is claiming to do something that only God can do. There is irony here, because what the Jewish theologians complain about is precisely part of the point. Even though they do not believe

20. Dunn, *Jesus Remembered*, 759–61.

21. Ladd, *Theology of the New Testament*, 156. As Goppelt (*Theology of the New Testament*, 186) states, "It is very probable, therefore, that Jesus himself made use of the Son of man concept as a model and filled it in such a way that it became a central expression of his mission." Later in his discussion (190–99), Goppelt explains that the association of death with the Messiah is unprecedented in Judaism, so the idea was not derived from Jesus's Jewish roots. He also speaks of Jesus's appropriation of Isa. 53 and declares that Mark 10:45 and Mark 14:24//Matt. 26:28 belong to the oldest strata of the tradition, suggesting their authenticity.

it, they correctly understand what Jesus is doing. In Mark 2 Jesus replies to the Jewish response by healing the paralytic, validating his original claim by using something that can be seen to explain what cannot be seen (Matt. 9:5–7//Mark 2:9–11//Luke 5:23–25). When Jesus claims to work alongside the Father on the Sabbath in John 5:1–18, he is claiming to make himself equal with God. Jesus's opponents appear to appreciate the significance of his actions and what they ultimately mean, but they reject him. So, with the awareness that Jesus's acts were highly controversial and could teach theology and Christology, we turn to his teaching and actions. For we hope to show that it is in Jesus's actions that he shows who he is.

5

Jesus's Teaching and Actions: Showing Who He Is

Pointing to His Unique Authority

To truly appreciate Jesus, it is imperative to understand his acts and their scope. Jesus highlighted who he was by *showing* who he was and discussing what his actions meant. Nothing illustrates the importance of this connection more than a text such as Matt. 11:2–6// Luke 7:21–23. When Jesus is asked directly by messengers of John the Baptist to confess whether he is "he who is to come," Jesus does not reply with an affirmative confession. Rather, he affirms his identity and the nature of the time by pointing to the acts that God is working through him, appealing to the language of the prophet Isaiah in the process (in order of mention: Isa. 29:18; 35:5–6; 42:18; 26:19; 61:1). The elements of the reply point to the activity of God in the new era of deliverance. Jesus answers the question positively by pointing to what God is doing through him.

This topic most helps us think through Jesus from the earth up in terms of the activity of Jesus's ministry. So we look to eleven different actions within Jesus's ministry that serve to testify to who he is and saw himself to be, many of which got him into trouble with the Jewish authorities and set the stage for his death.[1] Jesus's actions not only showed who he saw himself to be but also led the way to rejection of him by the Jewish leadership. Thus Jesus's actions were what forced one to decide what his ministry was and who was responsible for it.

Association with Tax Collectors and Sinners

We begin with one of the more relational and controversial aspects of Jesus's ministry: the way he opened himself up to the fringes of society, especially with those marked out as unrighteous.

Jesus's approach brought controversy because his ways were different from many of the pious within Second Temple Judaism. Here his actions stand in stark contrast to the community at Qumran, for example. That separatist society restricted access to God on the basis of ritual washings and a strict community code, including a long probationary period for prospective members. They had to prove their worth to be members of this community. Only those who rigorously kept the Torah could sit in God's presence. The Pharisees, though not as radical in their separatism as the Qumranians, also held to very restrictive access. And in the OT, access to the temple was restricted in such a way that those who were lepers or handicapped were denied. Although Jews were not unified in how they looked at sin and purity—the Qumranians often fused sin and impurity, while the Pharisees did not in some instances[2]—still the expectation was

1. For a consideration of what actions got Jesus into trouble, see Darrell L. Bock, "What Did Jesus Do That Got Him into Trouble? Jesus in the Continuum of Early Judaism–Early Christianity," in *Jesus in Continuum*, ed. Tom Holmén, WUNT 289 (Tübingen: Mohr Siebeck, 2012), 171–210. This essay places these events in their historical context and also discusses issues tied to authenticity. Actions covered that involved controversy include association with tax collectors and sinners, forgiveness of sins, Sabbath controversies, issues tied to purity, the temple incident, and the claim that God would vindicate him in resurrection to God's right hand. Acts of authority include exorcisms and redesigning liturgy.

2. On the Jewish views tied to sin, purity/impurity, and righteousness, see Jonathan Klawans, "Moral and Ritual Purity," in *The Historical Jesus in Context*, ed. A.-J. Levine, D. C. Allison Jr., and J. D. Crossan (Princeton: Princeton University Press, 2006), 266–84, esp. 278 and 281. In the OT, some impurity was simply the product of events in life (e.g., childbirth impurity tied to blood) rather than being about the presence of sin. So not all uncleanness was regarded as sin, though much of it was.

that righteousness led to the extending of grace, and the righteous were to maintain a distance from the unrighteous.

In contrast, Jesus sought out or was responsive to the unrighteous as well as the "impure."[3] Numerous texts report his controversial connections. His associations or positive examples in stories include tax collectors (Mark 2:17 par.; Luke 18:13; 19:7), a sinful woman (Luke 7:34, 37, 39), Samaritans (Luke 10:29–37), and even Gentiles (Matt. 15:21–28//Mark 7:24–30). His going to a banquet held by the tax collector Levi/Matthew (Matt. 9:9–13//Mark 2:13–17//Luke 5:27–32) led to his responding in terms of his mission of outreach as a physician coming to heal and call the sick. Luke adds the note that the call is to repentance. Jesus observes that his controversial associations have led some to reject him (Matt. 11:19//Luke 7:34). The parables of Luke 15 make a similar point, again explaining the associations in terms of seeking the lost. The call is to take the first steps toward those who are wandering and point them to God. Jesus's initiative to Zacchaeus (Luke 19:1–10) also belongs here. Also, Jesus's willingness to encounter lepers and the blind is part of this ministry emphasis. This portrait of Jesus is multiply attested and expresses one of the fundamental values of his ministry.

For Jesus, God was gracious in opening up access to those who would recognize their need for God and trust in him for spiritual care, like the way one might go to a doctor for physical care. He took the initiative in doing this and made the point emphatically by not requiring any formal restitution like the Qumranian probationary periods before becoming a full member of the righteous community.[4]

No story summarizes the difference in perspective as well as the story of the anointing of Jesus by the sinful woman in the house of Simon the Pharisee (Luke 7:36–50). The Pharisee makes the judgment

3. For a detailed examination of this theme, see Craig Blomberg, "The Authenticity and Significance of Jesus' Table Fellowship with Sinners," in *Key Events in the Life of the Historical Jesus: A Collaborative Exploration of Context and Coherence*, ed. Darrell L. Bock and Robert L. Webb (Tübingen: Mohr Siebeck, 2009), 215–50; and Blomberg's monograph *Contagious Holiness* (Downers Grove, IL: InterVarsity, 2005).

4. Although perhaps overdrawn in his criticism of other views that stressed grace alone as the issue, E. P. Sanders (*Jesus and Judaism* [Philadelphia: Fortress, 1985], 204–8) puts emphasis on the absence of any restitutionary requirements for entry in conjunction with repentance, a point that may well be correct.

that Jesus's willingness to associate with the woman disqualifies him from being a prophet. In contrast, Jesus argues that the potential of God forgiving a huge debt of sin drove him to reach out to her, so she could experience God's forgiveness.

This feature of Jesus's ministry challenged the portrait of who could belong to the community of God and also transformed the perception of how one gained righteousness. Did a person earn it, or did one receive it by grace? Was full transformation in practice required before entering into God's presence, or was this personal transformation a response of gratitude for having experienced God's grace? In contrast to the Jewish officials around him, Jesus emphasized access to God in the context of a gracious forgiveness available even to the most unrighteous. This acceptance of God's kindness was the ground for divine provision and transformation. So by his own authority and in distinction from surrounding tradition, Jesus defined whom God accepted. Such a definition of access to God by grace alone and the claim of authority over righteousness that it represented irritated the Jewish leadership.

Forgiveness of Sins

As much as Jesus's associations were an irritant to the leadership, his claim to be able to forgive sins was one of the major objections they had to his ministry. On this issue, two passages are key. One is the text of the sinful woman anointing Jesus (Luke 7:36–50). The other is the healing of the paralytic (Matt. 9:1–8//Mark 2:1–12//Luke 5:17–26). In both cases, the declaration of forgiveness of sins brings a reaction from the observers. In an irony of the text, the complaint by the theologians in these scenes is presented as an accurate reflection of the issue Jesus is raising. Only God forgives sin, but if this is so, then how can Jesus perform this act? The challenge of these two scenes is the same.

Since they question anyone being able to do this but God, those who raise the question have only two options. Either they believe that blasphemy has taken place in Jesus's assuming a prerogative that is God's alone (Mark 2:7 par.), or they raise a question about who he is because he speaks words of forgiveness (Luke 7:49). Although

Jesus does express the declaration with a passive idea ("Your sins are forgiven" [presumably by God]), his remarks are exceptional in that there is no declaration that God is responsible for this utterance, as in the case of Nathan to David in 2 Sam. 12:13 ("The Lord has taken away your sin," NASB). Nathan, speaking as a prophet for God, can make the remark, but he explicitly gives the credit for the declaration to God.[5] Jesus's declaration is less explicit about this affirmation that God forgives and thus represents a more direct claim, implying his own authority and making it more offensive to the leadership. It is this direct declaration that raises a problem for the Jewish leaders, who desire that God be acknowledged when sin is forgiven.

The question posed in Luke 7:49, then, is precisely that which the Scripture wishes to raise for reflection by Luke's reader: "Who is this, who even forgives sin?"[6] The question is posed but not answered at the literary level to allow reflection about the text. The scriptural portrait of Jesus makes forgiveness of sins one of the major irritants in the Jewish officials' reaction to Jesus. To them, he was claiming an exclusively divine prerogative. The irony of the text is that their observation about the significance of Jesus's act is accurate even as they reject it. If Jesus is able to forgive sin directly, then once again we have an act that raises the issue of how one should view Jesus, taking us from the earth up.

Sabbath Incidents and Healings

The issue of Jesus's healing on the Sabbath or of his disciples' breaking the Sabbath in other ways also produced controversy and raised

5. Discussion about whether a person can forgive sin in Judaism surrounds one Qumranian text, 4QPrNab 1.4 (= 4Q242), where forgiveness is mentioned. If this text declares that an exorcist forgave sin, then it is an exception to the rule in Judaism. No rabbinic texts make such an association. Whether this Qumran text refers to a declaration of forgiven sin ("an exorcist forgave my sin") or is a shorthand way to describe the effect of what the healing shows ("No one gets up from his sickbed until all his sins are forgiven" [*b. Ned.* 41a]) is not clear due to the fragmentary nature of the text.

6. What is important to remember about this question contextually is that the possibility of Jesus being a prophet had already been raised and rejected (Luke 7:39), so it looks as if some other role is implied by this question.

the question of Jesus's authority to act and interpret. Jesus is claiming authority over holy time and the divine calendar, with a promise rooted in the commandments. The Sabbath was a key distinctive within Judaism. Its observance was a point of piety and reflected covenant faithfulness. These actions must be seen in this light. Jesus is viewed as playing with a sacred day whose careful observance points to a faithful Jew.[7]

The key passage is a paired set of controversies in the Synoptic tradition that link the incidents of the plucking of grain on the Sabbath and the healing of the man with the withered hand (Mark 2:23–3:6// Matt. 12:1–14//Luke 6:1–11). The pairing of these two Sabbath events appears to belong to the early part of the tradition, because the healing of the man with the withered hand seems to confirm Jesus's remark that "the Son of Man is lord of the Sabbath." Jesus said this in order to defend the behavior of his disciples in plucking grain on the Sabbath.

In addition, Luke reports two other Sabbath healings (Luke 13:10–17, crippled woman; 14:1–6, man with dropsy). John also tells of healings on the Sabbath (John 5:1–18, man with paralysis; 7:22–23, looking back to John 5; 9:1–17, man born blind). So this kind of healing appears in three distinct layers of the Gospel tradition. As such, this kind of controversy is multiply attested across the tradition. Interestingly, the only two miracles that John's Gospel has in Jerusalem proper are these two Sabbath miracles.

Some challenge the authenticity of such events. They argue that there was no set Jewish tradition about Sabbath healing activity, that Jesus performed no real action in healing in the Mark 3:1–6 account (where he only speaks), and that the idea of Pharisees following Jesus

7. For a thorough treatment of this theme and its background in Second Temple Judaism, see Donald Hagner, "Jesus and the Synoptic Sabbath Controversies," in Bock and Webb, *Key Events in the Life of the Historical Jesus*, 251–92. Key OT texts for observance of the day are Exod. 20:8–11 and Deut. 5:12–15. A vivid Jewish text showing what was prohibited on the Sabbath is known as the "forty less one" (*m. Šabb.* 7.2). It lists thirty-nine things one cannot do on the Sabbath. A look at the Sabbath at Qumran, in the *Damascus Document*, and in the book of *Jubilees* shows how important the day was for many Jews. Also significant is the study by Christopher Tuckett, "Jesus and the Sabbath," in Holmén, *Jesus in Continuum*, 411–42.

and his disciples around in Galilee in the plucking-of-grain incident seems far-fetched.[8]

Key to this authenticity discussion and the reaction it brings is the recognition that the opposition to Jesus did not surface on the basis of only this one set of Sabbath actions. In other words, Jesus was performing many actions, such as forgiving sins and forgoing some traditional purity practices, that represented a challenge to the range of Jewish practice. The more Jesus made distinct challenges to different parts of Jewish traditional practice, the more each challenge became a part of the polemical environment that was forming. Part of the point of grouping all of Jesus's actions together in this section is to highlight at how many levels Jesus challenged current practice. Once he was viewed with suspicion and as the actions piled up, each action, no matter how seemingly minor initially, would be brought into the argument that Jesus was altering normal sacred customs. The authenticity challenge to Sabbath healing is possible only when critics again attempt to reject the evidence through a type of divide-and-conquer argument. A good case can be made for these scenes' authenticity.[9]

8. For such arguments, see Sanders, *Jesus and Judaism*, 264–67. More circumspect is John Meier, *A Marginal Jew: Rethinking the Historical Jesus*, 2 vols., ABRL (New York: Doubleday, 1994), 2:681–85, who doubts historicity and simply says that the case cannot be proved one way or the other, using many of the same arguments. The point about no set Jewish tradition is correct in that the Essenes of Qumran were stricter on Sabbath restrictions, not even allowing animals in desperate circumstances to be helped (CD 11.13–14), than were the Pharisees or the Sadducees (see *m. Šabb.* 18.3, where such help is permitted to animals except on a feast day). In the Jewish view of the healings expressed by the synagogue leader, since no life-or-death situation existed, the move to heal could wait a day (cf. Luke 13:14). Jesus's view was that a day given over to contemplating God was the best day for such a healing. See the discussions of the specific Jewish passages relating to these specific Synoptic texts in Darrell L. Bock, *Jesus according to Scripture: Restoring the Portrait from the Gospels* (Grand Rapids: Baker Academic, 2002).

9. Ben Witherington III, *The Christology of Jesus* (Minneapolis: Fortress, 1990), 66–73, defends the authenticity of the plucking-of-grain account. First, Witherington maintains that the setting connected to Abiathar, a controversial reference, does not look like a created detail. Second, that the controversy regarding the grain is about the disciples, not about Jesus, also counts against its being a made-up account: such a fictitious account, if it existed, would more likely be about Jesus directly. Third, there is no explicit development of the David-Jesus connection, so the alleged later Christology is too understated to be late. See also Graham Twelftree,

So what is the point of such incidents? What do they tell us about Jesus? Witherington summarizes well: "The categories of teacher or prophet are inadequate to explain such a stance: We have here either a lawbreaker or one who stands above the law and uses it to fit his mission and the new situation that results from that mission."[10]

That the topic swirls around one of the Ten Commandments underscores Jesus's claim to authority even more. For who has the authority to adjudicate over divinely authorized Torah commands? Although part of Jesus's answer in these disputes looks to the legal-ethical issues of the scope of the law in the face of acts of compassion or need, the final remark in the plucking-of-grain incident is a self-claim about Jesus's role. So Jesus's claim to be "lord" over the Sabbath is not the innocent remark of a prophet or an observation about the mere scope of the law in a dispute over practice. It is a claim to be the restorer of the kingdom presence of God with divine authority over how God's commands operate in that rule. In this way it is like the claim that the Son of Man also has authority to forgive sins (Mark 2:10).[11] Thus the portrait in John 5 that sees such an event as implying blasphemy is correct. Here is another act that was extremely irritating to those who read the law differently. It is another earth-up claim that is designed to have the reader reflect on who Jesus is.

Jesus the Miracle Worker: A Historical and Theological Study (Downers Grove, IL: InterVarsity, 1999), 295–97. With regard to Mark 3:1–6, Twelftree specifically challenges the claim that no work was done on the Sabbath in this healing by observing that the issue is not about an action that Jesus performs but about the fact that he acts to heal at all, by whatever means. Twelftree also states that the saying by itself makes no sense without the event that gives it contextual meaning. There is no indication that healing on the Sabbath was an early-church debate around which a story like this would be created. Most on target is the refutation by N. T. Wright (*Jesus and the Victory of God* [Minneapolis: Fortress, 1996], 390–96), who challenges Sanders's view directly and declares that the Pharisees were not "thought police" but more like self-appointed guardians of the Jewish culture. Texts such as Philo's *Spec. Laws* 2.46 §253 show the care with which some Jews brought oversight to the Sabbath. Jesus's kingdom claims and the prophetic nature of his ministry make his situation different in significance from the general practice of those who lived in Galilee. The Pharisees would have paid careful attention to him. Once Jesus was not seen as an ordinary Jew but as a threat, his actions would have been carefully watched.

10. Witherington, *Christology of Jesus*, 69.

11. So, correctly, Robert Gundry, *Mark: A Commentary on His Apology for the Cross* (Grand Rapids: Eerdmans, 1993), 144–45.

Exorcisms

The texts discussing exorcism include cleansing the demoniac in the synagogue (Mark 1:21–28//Luke 4:31–37), the Gerasene demoniac (Mark 5:1–20//Matt. 8:28–34//Luke 8:26–39), the Syrophoenician woman's daughter (Mark 7:24–30//Matt. 15:21–28), and the epileptic boy (Mark 9:14–29//Matt. 17:14–20//Luke 9:37–43). Interestingly, John's Gospel has no exorcisms. The exorcism accounts are reflected in the Markan strand of the tradition, with Matthew and Luke each using three of these accounts, but not the same three.[12] Numerous other texts assume such a ministry (Matt. 12:24//Luke 11:15//Mark 3:22; Luke 13:32; Mark 9:38–40//Luke 9:49–50; Matt. 9:32–33; Luke 8:2). Again, this theme is multiply attested across the tradition strands.

However, a final key text is a part of the Matthean-Lukan teaching tradition (Matt. 12:28//Luke 11:20). Matthew 12:24//Luke 11:15 makes clear that this healing of a mute man also is seen as an exorcism. This is a key text because it is a miracle account in form but in reverse of its normal emphases. Most miracle accounts spend the time on the details of the healing and note a reaction in passing. This text does the reverse. The miracle is briefly summarized, and then the reaction is where the account spends its time. The scene is designed to portray the significance of Jesus's healings as a whole and what the reaction was to them.

So what were the views that rotated around Jesus's activity? Some were open but skeptical, wanting to see more in a specific sign from heaven. Others already had an opinion. They claimed that Jesus healed by the power of Beelzebul, but Jesus explains it in a completely different way. Jesus acts by the power of God. In fact, Jesus goes through and argues that Satan healing is a contradiction in action. He works against himself, and if this is the case, his kingdom of doing destruction cannot stand. That leaves the action as explicable only as an act of God's presence and power.

12. For a defense of the historicity of this class of texts, see Twelftree, *Jesus the Miracle Worker*, 282–92. One should recall that even the Jewish materials recognized that Jesus performed such works, calling them "sorcery" (*b. Sanh*. 43a). Also, there is a thorough discussion on authenticity and Jewish background by Craig Evans, "Exorcisms and the Kingdom: Inaugurating the Kingdom of God and Defeating the Kingdom of Satan," in Bock and Webb, *Key Events in the Life of the Historical Jesus*, 151–79.

This text is important because it explains the significance of such healings in terms of the arrival of kingdom rule and authority. Jesus says, "If I cast out demons by the finger [Luke] / Spirit [Matthew] of God, then the kingdom of God has come upon you" (NASB). In both accounts this is followed by a parable where the house of a strong man (Satan) is plundered by a stronger man (Jesus), pointing to his victory over the forces of evil. Thus the exorcisms are graphic acts by Jesus to demonstrate that he has come to overturn the presence and authority of evil. More important than any theological debates that he may have with the Jewish leadership is his battle to overturn the hidden presence of evil, which shows itself in tearing down people. The exorcisms portray this battle in the most direct way. They also raise the question of who has the authority to exercise such power.

The Scope of Jesus's Miracles

In discussing miracles, we already have treated Sabbath healings and exorcisms. However, the array of Jesus's miraculous activity also should receive attention. There are nineteen miracle accounts in Mark alone, with a few summaries added to the list.[13] To this number Matthew adds two more: the healing of the official's son (8:5–13) and the catch of the coin in the mouth of the fish (17:24–27).[14] Luke also has twenty miracle stories and three summaries. He shares two of his miracles with the Matthean tradition of teaching (Luke 7:1–10; 11:14), and six miracles are unique to his Gospel: large catch of fish (5:1–11), raising of the widow of Nain's son (7:11–17), crippled woman healed on the Sabbath (13:10–17), man with dropsy healed on the Sabbath (14:1–6), ten lepers cleansed (17:11–19), and replacement of the severed ear of the high priest's servant (22:51).[15]

13. Twelftree, *Jesus the Miracle Worker*, 57. The texts are Mark 1:21–28, 29–31, 32–34 (summary), 40–45; 2:1–12; 3:1–6, 7–12; 4:35–41; 5:1–20, 21–43 (two miracles present); 6:30–44, 45–52, 53–56 (summary); 7:24–30, 31–37; 8:1–10, 22–26; 9:14–29; 10:46–52; 11:12–14 with 20–26. I count nineteen miracles here; Twelftree says there are twenty.

14. Ibid., 102.

15. Ibid., 144. In what follows, a text is described as "like" another if the passage is not clearly a true parallel yet may have a similar theme.

John has eight miracles: water changed to wine (2:1–12), healing of the official's sick son (4:46–54), healing of the paralytic at the pool (5:1–18), feeding of the five thousand (John 6:1–15//Mark 6:32–44// Matt. 14:13–21//Luke 9:10–17), Jesus walking on the water (John 6:16–21, like Mark 6:45–52//Matt. 14:22–33; cf. Mark 4:35–41//Matt. 8:23–27//Luke 8:22–25), restoring of sight to the man born blind (John 9:1–7), raising of Lazarus (11:1–57), and large catch of fish (21:4–14; like Luke 5:1–11). Josephus says that Jesus was a performer of "unusual" works (*Ant.* 18:63–64). Jesus's reputation as a healer is also acknowledged in the Jewish charge that he was a magician or sorcerer (Justin Martyr, *Dial.* 69.7; *b. Sanh.* 43a).[16] The charge by opponents does not accept him as working by God's power, but it does affirm that he is doing unusual things.

Besides exorcisms and healings that took place on the Sabbath, Jesus's healing miracles include healing paralytics, giving sight to the blind, curing lepers, raising the dead, curing fever, stopping a hemorrhage, making a deaf-mute speak and hear, reattaching a severed ear, and curing a man of dropsy. Nature miracles of another sort include two examples of a large catch of fish, catching a fish with a coin for tax, stilling a storm, feeding a multitude on two occasions, walking on water, turning water into wine, and withering a fig tree (the only miracle of judgment in the list). No other biblical figure has this scope of miraculous activity. The only other figures and periods that are close are the time of the exodus with Moses and the period of high apostasy countered by Elijah and Elisha. Only there do we see a combination of healing and exercise of authority over the elements. What these older parallels show is that the human figures could perform any one of these classes of miracle, although in the OT no one ever gives the blind sight. However, what is impressive is the scope of Jesus's activity, which involves the creation, the healing of the blind, the cleansing of lepers, and the power to raise from the dead. In this variety we see an authority that is unique in scope, a figure who is Moses's equal and much more.

16. For details on this Jewish tradition, see Graham Stanton, "Jesus of Nazareth: A Magician and a False Prophet Who Deceived God's People," in *Jesus of Nazareth: Lord and Christ; Essays on the Historical Jesus and New Testament Christology*, ed. Joel B. Green and Max Turner (Grand Rapids: Eerdmans, 1994), 164–80.

When given the chance to confess who he is, Jesus points to the miracles as his "witness" and explanation. Six texts are important here.

In Matt. 11:2–6//Luke 7:18–23, when John the Baptist sends a message asking if Jesus is "he who is to come," the miracle worker replies that John should be told what is being done: "The blind see, the lame walk, lepers are cleansed, the deaf hear, the dead are raised, and the good news is preached to the poor" (AT). Jesus replies in the language of hope—Isaiah's prophecies about the coming period of God's great work of salvation. The miracles being performed point out Jesus's identity and mission as well as the time of deliverance God has now brought.

The second and third texts come from John's Gospel, where Jesus's works attest to his claims (John 5:36; 10:38). They represent the work of the Father, authenticating the claims and person of Jesus. These Johannine texts that affirm the Son are fundamentally in agreement with Jesus's reply to John the Baptist. Such works show that Jesus can be trusted for what he says and claims.

The fourth text is associated with Jesus's nature miracles. After the stilling of the storm, the disciples ask themselves, "What sort of man is this that even winds and sea obey him?" (Matt. 8:27). The question is raised because the creation was seen to be in the hands of God (Job 40–42; Ps. 107:23–29). For a similar miracle in Matt. 14, where Jesus walks on the water, the resulting confession is combined with worship: "Truly you are the Son of God" (14:33). This miracle, showing Jesus's authority over creation, is another factor to consider when thinking about Jesus from the earth up.

The fifth text is tied to Jesus's power over life itself. This is most dramatically developed in the story of Lazarus, in which Jesus is portrayed as "the resurrection and the life" (John 11). Other resuscitation texts are Jairus's daughter (Matt. 9:18–26//Mark 5:21–43//Luke 8:40–56) and the widow of Nain's son (Luke 7:11–17). Being the source of life is yet another divine prerogative pointing to the earth up.

Finally, there is a sequence of texts in Mark 4:35–5:43//Luke 8:22–56. Here the scope of Jesus's miraculous power is summarized in a linked series of four miracles: calming of the sea, exorcism, healing of a woman with a hemorrhage, and a raising from the dead. This sequence covers the whole scope of Jesus's power, from creation to supernatural forces, human well-being, and life itself. It goes from decree over creation to defeating demons, disease, and death. It shows that Jesus has the power to deliver, and to do so comprehensively. It also raises the question of what human being is like this.

Thus the scope of the miracles indicates the comprehensive extent of Jesus's authority. The power over life, demons, and the creation indicates a scope of authority in one person that can exist only because he shares in divine power. Again we summarize from another study of the topic. Graham Twelftree concludes his study of Jesus's miracles with this note: "In short, for Jesus and the Gospel writers, a miracle performed by Jesus is an astonishing event, exciting wonder in the observers, which carries the signature of God, who, for those with the eye of faith, can be seen to be expressing his powerful eschatological presence."[17]

Purity and Other Practices

This issue involves mainly two texts (Mark 7:1–23//Matt. 15:1–20). These are the only Gospel texts where the question of what is "common" or "profane" (κοινός [i.e., unclean]) comes up. Pharisees and scribes challenge Jesus for the disciples' failure to keep "the tradition of the elders." They fail to wash their hands to prevent uncleanness in their handling of food.[18] Other texts address Jesus's practice in relationship to fasting or point to Jesus's critique of the religious practices of the Jewish leaders (Luke 5:33–39; 11:37–54//Matt. 23:1–39). These texts do not so much challenge purity practices as reprioritize them, making true piety a reflection of more than one's ability to follow detailed practices on the basis of specific legal stipulations.

In Matt. 15:1–20 Jesus replies in kind, declaring that the tradition of the Pharisees and scribes breaks the ethical side of the law by violating the command to honor mother and father. In doing this, Jesus

17. Twelftree, *Jesus the Miracle Worker*, 350.

18. For discussion of the Jewish practice here, see Roger Booth, *Jesus and the Laws of Purity: Tradition History and Legal History in Mark 7*, JSNTSup 13 (Sheffield: JSOT Press, 1986), 155–87.

is not allowing the stipulations of the law to be interpreted on their own apart from other scriptural considerations. Scripture is not to be read in isolation from topic to topic but as a whole. This leads to his prioritizing the pieces so that the relational elements of the law are not denied but practiced. Jesus goes on to assert that it is not what goes into a person that defiles but what comes out of the mouth. When the disciples see that the Pharisees are offended by his statements, Jesus drives the point home: "Every plant which *my* heavenly Father has not planted will be rooted up" (Matt. 15:12–13). Then he calls the Pharisees "blind guides" (15:14). Jesus's final remark on the topic is that what comes out of the mouth and out of the heart is what defiles, "but to eat with unwashed hands does not defile" (15:20).

Mark goes a similar route, even describing the customs for his Gentile audience in 7:3–4. When asked, Jesus challenges the critics for their hypocrisy with regard to honoring mother and father. Then he tells the crowd that what defiles is not what comes from outside but what comes out of a person. In Mark, Jesus stresses that what emerges from the heart defiles a person. Mark alone also adds the implication of Jesus's remarks (although this was not immediately recognized): Jesus "declared all foods clean" (7:19). With this reflective remark, Mark presents Jesus's teaching as the beginning of turning a corner on the stipulations of the law. His presentation is more radical than Matthew, who lets the event speak for itself without pursuing any implications of the scene. Matthew's concern for his predominantly Jewish-rooted audience may also be at work here.

All of this tradition was developed from Lev. 15, where being made unclean by a discharge required a washing. Although the body was still considered unclean for a time after the washing, a rinsing rendered the hands clean.

What Jesus responds to, then, is the tradition built around uncleanness, including the biblical call for love and a pure heart, not just the Torah per se. Jesus's response makes clear that he rejected the use of oral law, which, with its extra requirements beyond Scripture, was said to build a fence around Torah. However, when Jesus goes on to elaborate his response, he does comment on matters of "defiling" that Torah does treat. He opts for a priority on the ethical dimensions of the law, stressing personal behavior. Both the rebuke that confronts them on how parents are dishonored and the emphasis on defiling coming from the heart show this focus on the law as it relates to one's interpersonal actions. When Mark adds the narrative comment that the effect of Jesus's remarks was to make all foods clean (7:19), he shows Jesus's emphasis by reconfiguring how the law is seen and prioritizing it in relationship to other scriptural themes. Reading Matthew gives one the same sense, but to a lesser degree. The emphasis on the interpersonal relationships is still there, but the explicit statement of foods being declared clean is lacking.

Jesus's comments are not merely those of a prophet commenting on the law, nor are they the work of a scribe interpreting the law. Jesus does not argue as later rabbis did, citing the precedent of other rabbinic opinions. Rather, the point is that Jesus, in light of his authority, has the right to comment and even to prioritize matters tied to purity. Ben Meyer speaks of an "eschatological ethic" at work here as the arrival of the new age brings a fresh look at the law and its priorities: a standard of righteousness to which the law always aimed is being more effectively worked out in conjunction with the promise of the new era.[19] Jesus's remark in defense of his lack of fasting—that new wine requires new wineskins—makes the point explicitly (Mark 2:22// Matt. 9:17//Luke 5:38). This kind of supersession also must point to the revealer. As Meyer states, "Since the Mosaic code was conceived to have been divinely revealed, any code claiming to supersede it had somehow to include the claim to be equally revealed—indeed, to belong to a superior revelation."[20] The new era promised in Jer. 31:32–33 was not to be like the one revealed on the mountain. The law would be lodged in the heart by being written there.

This also had implications for the revelator. Who could emphasize and reveal the scope of the law and practice that God gave through Moses in this fresh way? It is someone through whom God brought a time that transcended that of Moses and who transcended Moses himself. Here Jesus did not claim to go up the mountain to get the revelation of God as Moses had. Rather, he spoke directly of what

19. Ben Meyer, *The Aims of Jesus* (London: SCM, 1979), 138–39. He goes on to say, "Jesus was not a rabbi but a prophet and, like John, 'more than a prophet.' He was the unique revealer of the full final measure of God's will" (151).

20. Ibid., 152.

"*my* Father" would do and what he requires. There is a directness to this sending and revealing. Thus these acts inherently present a claim of authority and divine insight. Purity and fasting were not the only areas tied to the law and handled in this way by Jesus.

Law Issues

In one sense, this section is an extension of the previous ones. We have already looked at issues tied to the Sabbath, to purity, and to fasting, which are legal matters. Also relevant are matters tied to the temple. However, that discussion is important enough on its own terms to be covered separately later. This subunit considers all other matters related to the law not found in the other subunits treating legal questions.

The portrait of the law in the Gospels varies in emphasis, depending on the Gospel.[21] The term "law" (νόμος) never appears in Mark, but it is used 8 times in Matthew (5:17, 18; 7:12; 11:13; 12:5; 22:36, 40; 23:23), 4 times in Luke 10–24 (10:26; 16:16, 17; 24:44) plus 5 times in Luke 2 (vv. 22, 23, 24, 27, 39), and 15 times in John (1:17, 45; 7:19 [2×], 23, 49, 51; 8:5, 17; 10:34; 12:34; 15:25; 18:31; 19:7 [2×]).

Mark's handling of the law appears to be the most radical in that he develops Jesus's break with the law in the most explicit terms. This emphasis especially surfaces in his unique narrative remark about how Jesus declared all food clean (Mark 7:19).[22] Matthew and Luke are more restrained. With Mark, they share several texts that show Jesus following the law (e.g., Matt. 8:1–4//Mark 1:40–45//Luke 5:12–16), while also noting the tension of prioritizing ethical dimensions over the cultic in his remarks and acts of Sabbath healing (in remarks unique to Matthew, Matt. 9:13; 12:7; in Markan tradition, Matt. 12:1–8//Mark 2:23–28//Luke 6:1–5; Matt. 12:9–14//Mark 3:1–6//Luke 6:6–11; so also John 4:22–24). This is a multiply attested theme.

21. For this subject area, see William R. G. Loader, *Jesus' Attitude towards the Law*, WUNT 2/97 (Tübingen: Mohr Siebeck, 1997).

22. There is a textual problem in Mark 7:19, but the bulk of the best manuscripts read a remark that should be seen as a narrative comment by Mark.

In the Sabbath healings, Jesus mentions that David violated the rules when he ate the sacred bread. Jesus's observation that David was not judged for violating the letter of the law makes his point about ethical priority.

In the Gospels, the temple is discussed in a way that both implies its removal (John 2:19–22) and looks to its role as a place of prayer not to be defiled (Matt. 21:12–13//Mark 11:15–18//Luke 19:45–46; Matt. 5:23–24; 23:16–22). This second type of saying also looks to the ethical dimensions of how worship should be evaluated.

John's Gospel tends to portray the period of the law as past and its feasts as realized in Jesus (John 1:17). Also, John often cites the law as testifying to what Jesus is experiencing, as a text where the mission of Christ is discussed or attested, or as a text that explains how Jesus should be treated (John 1:45; 8:17; 12:34; 15:25; 18:31; 19:7).

Luke and Matthew also have remarks that go in this direction, where the period of the kingdom follows that of the law and prophets as its fulfillment (Matt. 11:13//Luke 16:16). The new era brings new realities, as the saying on the new wineskins argues (Mark 2:18–22// Matt. 9:14–17//Luke 5:33–39). The image of celebrating the groom's presence also points to the arrival of the new era. Yet Jesus does not do away with fasting here. He simply says other factors make the current time not appropriate for it. The arrival of the new era calls for celebration.

Outside of these generalized texts, two passages are especially important: (1) the text about the greatest commandment (Mark 12:28–34//Matt. 22:34–40; like Luke 10:25–28 and 18:18–20, where the relational dimension of the Ten Commandments is discussed in response to a question about how to receive eternal life) and (2) the six antitheses (Matt. 5:21–48), a text unique to Matthew.

The ethical prioritization noted in the discussion on purity shows up in the "great commandment" text. Here the law is distilled to love for God and love for one's neighbor. Certain Jewish texts made similar comments.[23] Jesus upholds the law in its relational emphasis, making the point that our relationship to God should impact how

23. Some of these texts are disputed as having been influenced by Christian interpolations (*T. Dan* 5.3; *T. Iss.* 5.2; 7.6). However, Philo, *Spec. Laws* 2.15 §63, makes a similar emphasis. The roots of this are in the prophets (Mic. 6:8; Isa. 33:15–16;

others are treated as well. Matthew 22:40 expresses it by saying that the law and the prophets hang on these emphases, like hinges that make a door workable. In Matt. 23:23 Jesus rebukes the Pharisees for their failure to apply the law in this relational way. Their error is that they treat the law simply as a string of commands. John 13:34 seems to go in a similar direction with a "new commandment" to love one another. Jesus highlights this at his last meal with the disciples.

These texts set a tone about the one who participates in the new era. This tone is that love for God also expresses itself in love for others. So repentance in Luke is presented even in the preparatory work of John the Baptist, which involves a relational reshuffling that brings fathers back to children and the disobedient back to the pious (Luke 1:16–17). The same linkage is reflected when those responding to John ask what they must do to show deeds worthy of repentance (Luke 3:10–14). In each case, the presentation does not make an appeal to some aspect of worship, law, or elements tied to a walk with God, but to how one relates to others. In other words, this emphasis is seen in multiple layers of the early Christian tradition about the emergence of this movement and its priorities.

Equally revealing are the antitheses of the Sermon on the Mount (Matt. 5:21–48). Sometimes it is argued that Jesus is merely rejecting oral law in his "you have heard it said, but I say to you" remarks (5:21, 27, 33, 38, 43). In part this position is taken because Jesus introduces the antitheses with the remark that he came to fulfill the law and the prophets and that one should not teach anything that alters a jot or tittle of the law (Matt. 5:17–20). This argument does not work. Verse 20 makes clear that one's righteousness is to exceed that of the scribes and Pharisees, not be a different type of righteousness. Jesus then expounds what this means in the antitheses. So the result is that this exceeding righteous standard comes from reading the law not for its letter but for what it asks of the heart, as all the following examples show.

The antitheses intensify each command, pressing it in terms of its internal intent. So the issue is not just murder but also anger that

cf. Ps. 15). Rabbi Hillel taught, "What seems to you to be hurtful, do not to your neighbor; that is the whole Torah. All the rest is commentary" (*b. Šabb.* 31a).

leads to murder. The issue is not just adultery but also lust that leads to adultery. The issue is not thinking through how one can get out of marriage, but taking one's vow seriously in order to keep it, recognizing also that God is involved in bringing a couple together. The issue is not how an oath is worded, but the integrity that makes oath taking unnecessary. The issue is not eye-for-eye retribution, but a kind of nonretaliation that keeps the spiral of violence from spinning out of control.[24] This example is particularly revealing, showing Jesus's emphasis on the relational dimension of the law and a refocus on a fresh hub for it, so that relationships do not break down. Absence of retribution again is the point in Jesus's stepping back from the call to hate one's enemy. The standard may not be what is "fair" or "equal," but what goes beyond the call of normal duty to reverse the cycle that causes relationships to be destroyed. The outcome is clear: the standard of righteousness that Jesus's reading of the law calls for exceeds that of the scribes and Pharisees. Jesus's standard operates at a higher level than the one the world or the Jewish teachers live by. It reflects the character of God in the process; for in the call to show mercy and love, the example of God is invoked, and those who live this way are called sons and daughters of God (cf. Matt. 5:45).

So Jesus's remarks in Matt. 5:17–20 about coming to fulfill the law must be read in this light. Here Jesus is not discussing a casuistic consideration of legal detail and scribal ruling, but a reading that looks at the scope and inner goal of the law to enhance relationships and reflect God's gracious character and righteousness. In this holistic reading of Scripture, stipulations are seen for where they direct the heart, not just for ascertaining the minimum requirement to avoid being accused of a violation.

A final text tied to the law is where Jesus discusses marriage as a result of a question raised by the Pharisees (Matt. 19:1–9//Mark 10:1–9). While the Pharisees wanted to know about what justifies a divorce, Jesus stressed that the commitment of marriage between one man and one woman involves fulfilling the oath of promise the couple made to each other, while recognizing that God has joined

24. Note how this antithesis simply cites Exod. 21:24 or Lev. 24:20. There is no oral law mentioned here.

them together. This reading also focuses on the character and intent of the law: marriage vows should be honored and kept. It is only "hardness of heart" that creates divorce.

All of this raises questions: Who has the authority to open up the inner character of the law in this way? Who gets to discern what is to be kept and what is less important? Who decides when certain legal limitations apply and when they do not? There is an authority here over the law that raises questions about who it is who reveals this interpretation of the law. Again, a quotation from Witherington pulls all the strands of this section together:

> Jesus seems to assume an authority over Torah that no Pharisee or Old Testament prophet assumed—the authority to set it aside. What is striking is that his response in the authentic material seems varied. Sometimes he affirms the validity of some portions of the law. Sometimes he intensifies the law's demands (e.g., portions of the Sermon on the Mount), a point of view that does not violate the law but goes beyond it. Sometimes he adds new material, apparently of juridical force to the law (e.g., his teaching on adultery and divorce in Mark 10//Matthew 19). Sometimes he sets aside Torah as he does in Mark 7:15. In short, he feels free not only to operate with a selective hermeneutic but also to add and subtract from Scripture. All of this suggests that Jesus did not see himself as a Galilean Hasid ["holy man"] or another prophet, even one like Elijah. He saw himself in a higher or more authoritative category than either of these types familiar to Jewish believers.[25]

This summary is well stated and correctly surfaces the question of what kind of person Jesus saw himself to be in claiming and assuming such authority. Jesus had no doubt that he could serve as the revelator of God, speaking and revealing the divine way and will. He and the Father were one when it came to understanding what law and divine will required. Jesus's response in John 5 to the "breaking" of the Sabbath proceeds in exactly this way. So does the claim to be "lord of the Sabbath." Once again, John's Gospel is shown to be conceptually parallel to what the Synoptics reveal, even though the form of

25. Witherington, *Christology of Jesus*, 65.

expression differs. Jesus's attitude to the law set a direction that later was taken up in the early church's insistence that circumcision was not required for Gentile believers, even though it had been so central a sign in the law tied to the founding Abrahamic covenant. It took awhile for this emphasis to make itself clear to them, as Acts 10–15 testifies. How Jesus handled the law is another example of actions revealing Jesus from the earth up. The handling of God's law in this way reflects divine prerogatives. The scope of how Jesus did it points in the same direction.

So two key points also are clear from Jesus's teaching on the law. (1) The law was designed to form compassion and character. The law needed to be read with an eye to where it takes us relationally. Unique to Matthew, Jesus's statement that God desires mercy and not sacrifice summarizes this emphasis (Matt. 9:13; 12:7). The point is that mercy is more central than sacrifice, though both are asked for. In this way Jesus shows how he handled legal questions and did so with a scriptural emphasis. (2) Jesus's reading of the law shows his authority over it. If I may paraphrase, it shows that the Son of Man is not simply lord of the Sabbath; he also is lord over the reading of the law. In this, Jesus reveals not only his authority but also his wisdom as the interpreter of the law par excellence. Jesus functions here as Word and revelator.

Redesigning Liturgy

Underscoring what has been said about the law is how Jesus handles sacred liturgy rooted in the law, as evidenced by the Last Supper (Matt. 26:17–30//Mark 14:12–26//Luke 22:7–23). What appears to be a Passover meal is reinterpreted in terms of Jesus's approaching death (Mark 14:12 with 22–24; Luke 22:15). At least we have a meal offered during Passover season that evokes the establishing of a new relationship with God on terms that Jesus creates. The connection to Passover imagery is likely, given that they are eating the meal as Jerusalem pilgrims there for Passover, even if we cannot be absolutely sure that a Passover meal was the occasion.[26] A sacred meal, or at least

26. There is debate whether a Passover meal is at the base of the Last Supper, although this does seem likely. Even if it is not, the event took place so close to Passover

imagery tied to a sacred event, the exodus, is completely reshaped into a message about the new era of eschatological deliverance.[27]

So what does this recasting in terms of sacrifice and covenant show about Jesus? The remarks about the meal clearly present Jesus as a sacrifice who opens up the way to the new covenant relationship with God. According to Luke and Paul, Jesus's sacrifice, as represented in the cup, established the "new covenant in my blood" (Luke 22:20//1 Cor. 11:25).[28] Jesus is the means through which forgiveness is given on the basis of that death. That this result is associated with the kingdom is clear from Jesus's remark about not drinking of the cup again until he drinks it anew in the kingdom of God. The bread-and-cup imagery emphasizes the issues tied to what Jesus provides through his death (establishing a covenant, offering forgiveness). Jesus then stands at the hub or base of a new era and makes provision for establishing a fresh way of relating to God in a fresh context of forgiveness. Both the bread and the cup picture what Jesus offers "on your behalf." The blood pictures what is "poured out for many" (Matt. 26:28//Mark 14:24). Here Isa. 53:12 stands in the background, while the Passover stands as the illustrative event. Just as blood on the doorposts covered and protected the Israelite families when the tenth

---

that the associations would exist. The classic work arguing for a Passover meal is Joachim Jeremias, *The Eucharistic Words of Jesus*, trans. N. Perrin, 2nd ed., New Testament Library (New York: Scribner, 1966). In contrast stands the thesis of Bruce Chilton, who argues that the Passover connection is anachronistic and instead sees the meal in terms of Jesus's view of cultic purity and his practice of forgiveness, as seen in his meals and associations: *The Temple of Jesus: His Sacrificial Program within a Cultural History of Sacrifice* (University Park: Pennsylvania State University Press, 1992), 148–54. This approach seems to me to ignore the background inevitably raised by the festal occasion, regardless of what we can or cannot know exactly about the form of a Passover meal at the time. To speak of a death at Passover time in the context of a work of deliverance naturally would lead to this association. Thus a Passover backdrop is still more likely here. So Leonhard Goppelt, *Theology of the New Testament*, ed. Jürgen Roloff, trans. John E. Alsup (Grand Rapids: Eerdmans, 1981), 215. In this way, Passover as a season worked for Jews much as Christmas for our culture is about more than one day and one specific ceremony.

27. For other details about the event, see the discussion in Bock, *Jesus according to Scripture*. Here our concern is the import of the event.

28. Matthew 26:28 and Mark 14:24 speak only of the "blood of the covenant," but the fact that a covenant is established by the shedding of blood means a new covenant is being inaugurated. Luke and Paul write "new covenant" and thus make explicit what Matthew and Mark leave implicit. All four make the same point.

plague roamed through Egypt and led to the nation's deliverance, so Jesus's death covers and provides a way of salvation for those who share in covenantal faith. The meal was a promise that what Jesus was to do would provide a context for a new relationship with God, which had been promised long ago.[29]

That Jesus could take sacred exodus imagery and refill it speaks to his view as interpreter of both God's law and plan. It also points to his ability to take on a creative role in that plan, to author and perfect a traditional act of worship. He acts as the unique sent revelator of God. It is like the authority he exercised over the law. It is also like the authority he asserts in the temple. Jesus is expanding and reshaping most of the major images of Judaism. All of this activity raises a chief question: What sort of person is able to recast old sacred rites?[30] Jesus is not merely establishing a new rite; he is modifying one of the most sacred rites of Israel, a rite tied to the nation's origin. Jesus's belief that he can do this shows how in tune he was with God's way and will.

Temple and Temple Cleansing

Jesus displayed a mixed relationship to the temple in his various remarks and activities associated with it. In many ways, that mix is much like his approach to issues of law in general. Some things are affirmed, while other remarks show that the temple would not remain the center of activity that it had been.

It is debated whether Jesus's act in clearing out the temple's money changers was a call of cleansing reform for the temple or a symbolic

29. When one adds the portrait of John's Gospel here, the results are interesting. John does not depict the Last Supper with its bread and cup, but what he does highlight is the announcement of the coming of the Paraclete (the Holy Spirit), yet another key dimension of the new-covenant promise. John's role in supplementing well-known tradition is seen here. He also alludes to eating bread and drinking blood in John 6, showing that he is aware of the meal and its representative symbolism pointing to covenant life.

30. Goppelt, *Theology of the New Testament*, 220, says it this way: "Jesus now vouchsafed forgiving fellowship by giving himself as the One who died for the benefit of all others. It is not a heavenly body, not a pneumatic substance, that was given, and also not only an atoning power, but Jesus as the One who died for all."

picture of its destruction (John 2:13–22; Matt. 21:12–13//Mark 11:15–17//Luke 19:45–46).[31] A good case can be made for each option.

In favor of a symbolic act picturing destruction are (1) the following fig tree incident, in which the cursed and later destroyed fig tree represents, according to this view, the temple as a symbol of the nation's unique connection to God; (2) the remarks of John 2:19, which suggest a concern about another temple more important to God's plan than the physical temple—namely, Jesus himself; and (3) in the Olivet Discourse, Jesus's predictions of the temple's coming destruction (Matt. 24//Mark 13//Luke 21:5–37). This view appeals to other events in the context that suggest the importance of Jesus's action in the temple.

However, in support of a cleansing reform are the remarks about the temple within this passage. This includes the idea of the temple being designed to be either a place of prayer (Matt. 21:13) or a place for the nations to pray (Mark 11:17). This appears to foresee a time when the temple will continue to function. In addition, the early church kept its attachment to the temple, so any idea that it ceased to have value or was totally obsolete appears not to have been adopted by the church.

The Jewish background that the temple would be part of what would be renewed in the last times also is part of the backdrop of

31. For the destruction view, see Wright, *Jesus and the Victory of God*, 413–28; for that of destruction with the expectation of a renewed temple, see Sanders, *Jesus and Judaism*, 61–76; for the view "more probably" of a symbolic cleansing as a messianic act tied to entry, see Witherington, *Christology of Jesus*, 107–16. As the above studies show, even more disputed is why the cleansing/destruction was required. Was it for economic reasons (Sadducees taking unfair economic advantage), purity reasons (sacrifices did not really belong to the worshiper but were merely purchased, or sacrifices were moved into the holy space of the court of the Gentiles), both, or the temple as a symbol for Israel's nationalism? This is less than clear, although I prefer the option that both economic and worship ideals were being compromised by the recent move of the money changers into the court. See earlier discussion of the passage. Meyer, *Aims of Jesus*, 197, rightly calls it several things: a demonstration, a prophetic critique, a fulfillment event, and a sign of the future. The temple cleansing pledges the "perfect restoration of Israel" (198). A full treatment of this event, including issues tied to authenticity, comes from Klyne Snodgrass, "The Temple Incident," in Bock and Webb, *Key Events in the Life of the Historical Jesus*, 429–80. He argues for a mix of cleansing and destruction, with more emphasis on cleansing. In Jesus's act "was a prophetic protest that pointed to future eschatological hope" (471).

Jesus's action, pointing slightly more to a cleansing (*1 En.* 90.28–30, 40; Zech. 14:21; Shemoneh Esreh, benediction 14). These factors appear to suggest that the temple was being cleansed with a prophetic-like call to the nation to behave appropriately in the temple. There is no doubt that if covenantal unfaithfulness continued, then judgment would come (Mark 13:2//Matt. 24:2//Luke 21:5–6; Luke 13:34–35// Matt. 23:37–39). However, it is better to see Jesus acting as a messianic claimant bringing eschatological renewal. He is making his statement about the need for reform of the temple to prepare for the new era. This is like the prayer in benediction 14 of Shemoneh Esreh, which links messianic hope and the temple, just as the later inquiry of Jesus before the council moves from temple to messiahship. It also reflects the picture of *Pss. Sol.* 17–18 that the messiah to come would purge Jerusalem, cleanse it, and make it righteous. The fact that this is Jesus's first act after entering the city as a messianic claimant also makes this connection to Messiah's coming and claiming to purge the temple likely.[32] If this claim meets with rejection, then the nation stands culpable.

Again, to make such a move by itself could have been seen as merely prophetic, but placed alongside the other eschatological claims of Jesus and his other actions that touched on the law, a more messianic claim surfaces with implications for the kingdom's arrival. Jesus is challenging the management of holy space by what he does here. The temple is Israel's most sacred spot and the most holy place on earth for a Jew. To see oneself as having the authority to exercise judgment over the central religious symbol of the nation and the most sacred spot in the world was to perform an act that assumed a claim to divinely connected authority. It is another earth-up act.

This is precisely why the cleansing raises the leaders' question after the event about the source of Jesus's authority (Matt. 21:23–27//Mark 11:27–33//Luke 20:1–8). It was exactly the right question to raise. Even the way Jesus plays with the "temple" image, fusing his body as temple with the physical temple, suggests a level of holiness associated with his presence that links it to God's presence (John 2:19, 21). So,

32. For a detailed consideration of the significance and authenticity of Jesus's entry into Jerusalem, see Brent Kinman, "Jesus' Royal Entry into Jerusalem," in Bock and Webb, *Key Events in the Life of the Historical Jesus*, 383–427.

like the handling of the law, the treatment of the temple suggests an authority over the most sacred of Israel's sites, the very place where God dwells. Jesus is the Messiah and, more than the temple, functions as the hub of what the promise brings in needed restructuring.

Suffering and Cross

In this section we consider what Jesus had to say about his rejection and suffering. The narrative depictions of the cross do not fit here, since they are presented in terms of the evangelists' understandings of the event. In general, these depictions portray Jesus as a righteous sufferer, along the lines of the psalms, or as an innocent man sent to his death even though the one judging him (Pilate) is not truly convinced of his guilt. Luke emphasizes this innocence theme, and it is present also in Matthew and John.[33]

The passion predictions speak of the necessity of Jesus's suffering or of fulfilling Scripture (Mark 8:31//Matt. 16:21//Luke 9:22; Mark 14:21// Matt. 26:24; Luke 18:31; 22:22). In particular in Mark, Jesus suffers as the Son of Man. The idea of Jesus being handed over (παραδιδόναι) appears to recall Isa. 53:6, 12 (Mark 9:31//Matt. 17:22//Luke 9:44; Mark 10:33//Matt. 20:18).[34] This probably represents a fusion of exalted Son of Man background with the suffering of the righteous and the Servant images.[35] Also important is the imagery of Zech. 9–14, in which the

33. In Matthew, Pilate washes his hands and is warned by his wife after she has a dream. As in the infancy material, dreams play a major role in Matthew, showing God's involvement in the events. See John 18:38; 19:4.

34. Joel Marcus, *The Way of the Lord: Christological Exegesis of the Old Testament in the Gospel of Mark* (Louisville: Westminster/John Knox, 1992), 193–94.

35. On the background and authenticity of these suffering Son of Man sayings, see Darrell L. Bock, *Luke 1:1–9:50*, BECNT (Grand Rapids: Baker, 1994), 952–55; Hans Bayer, *Jesus' Predictions of Vindication and Resurrection: The Provenance, Meaning and Correlation of Synoptic Prediction*, WUNT 2/20 (Tübingen: Mohr Siebeck, 1986). The key texts here appear to be Ps. 118; Isa. 53; and the suffering righteous in the Psalter, appealing to passages such as Pss. 22; 31; and 69, which show up in Jesus's utterances on the cross. In this portrait, the utterances of Jesus in Mark and Matthew have a note of lament through Ps. 22:1, while Luke's Jesus sounds a note of trust and hope of triumph in the use of Ps. 31:5. All the Gospels, including John, have imagery from Ps. 69. Texts speaking to the vindication of the righteous may also have a role (OT: Pss. 3; 8; 9; 18; 27; 32; 56; other Jewish texts: Wis. 2:12–20; 5:1–7).

shepherd is struck and the sheep are scattered (Mark 14:27).[36] These predictions possess three basic elements: (1) rejection as seen in the delivering over, (2) death, and (3) vindication in a quick resurrection.

The theme of rejection-vindication also is seen in the use of Ps. 118:22, which appears in two contexts, one tied to the parable of the wicked tenants (Matt. 21:42//Mark 12:10–11//Luke 20:17) and another associated with Jesus's warning about Israel's coming desolation (Luke 13:34–35). Here the rejected stone becomes the exalted stone, which also is a stumbling stone. Psalm 118 is too little appreciated for what it has to say about vindication and suffering-to-exaltation themes in the NT. It is a text that appears in many Gospel passages.

Similar in implication is the appeal to Ps. 110:1, which comes to be read as about the vindication of a judged Jesus. In that vindication, Jesus is raised to a seat at God's right hand, despite being sentenced to death (Matt. 26:64//Mark 14:62//Luke 22:69). In other words, most of the Gospel texts concentrate on the fact that Jesus as a righteous one was unjustly crucified, but that God would reverse the injustice into exaltation and victory. The reversal is seen as divine substantiation for Jesus's claims.

The theme of Isa. 53, though its presence here has been debated, also is not absent.[37] Four texts are especially pertinent to arguing that all of Isa. 40–66 is important to Mark's understanding. They are Mark 9:12, about suffering and being despised, appealing to Isa. 53:3; the passion predictions as a group, appealing to Isa. 53:8 (on judgment) and 53:6, 12 (on being handed over); Mark 10:45, with the concept of ransom tied conceptually to Isa. 53:12; and Mark 14:22–24, about bearing the sins of many with poured-out blood, appealing to Isa. 53:12b (also Matt. 26:27–28). Again, most of these texts simply describe the circumstances of rejection. However, the reference to ransom and to blood being poured out for many begins to describe how forgiveness is achieved. Here the seeds for the theology of Jesus's work on the cross are found. Mark 14:22–24, set in the backdrop of

36. Marcus, *The Way of the Lord*, 157.

37. The debate is reflected in the essays in William H. Bellinger and William R. Farmer, eds., *Jesus and the Suffering Servant: Isaiah 53 and Christian Origins* (Harrisburg, PA: Trinity Press International, 1998). The essay by Morna Hooker argues against such a connection, while essays by Otto Betz and Rikki Watts argue for it.

Passover, also underscores this sacrificial, substitutionary, deliverance context, as we argued in discussing the liturgy of the Last Supper. Luke 22:37 also appeals to language of the Servant portrait in Isa. 53:12 to describe the depth of the rejection. This righteous one is viewed as a "lawless" one, a transgressor.

These texts show Jesus as portraying the experience of the cross in many dimensions. He is rejected and regarded as unrighteous, yet he is an innocent sufferer. The actual descriptions of Jesus's death on the cross and the Scripture he cites from the cross point to this portrait. The injustice of the cross will be vindicated when Jesus is raised up like the rejected stone of Ps. 118:22–23. John's Gospel also supports this idea when it speaks of the Son of Man being lifted up. Here the cross is seen not as a defeat but as the means of glorification for the Son (John 3:14; 17:1–5). Neither Jesus nor the evangelists say much in describing how forgiveness comes through Jesus's work, but the texts that do treat it view his death as a sacrifice, opening up the way to a new covenant. In a larger context, this prepares for the coming of the Spirit, the sign of the new age (John 14–16).

Thus, in terms of Christology, Jesus's suffering and cross mark him out as one whom God vindicates even as he suffers an unjust and heinous death born out of rejection. He suffers primarily as the Son of Man, but the portrait is drawn from texts depicting the righteous sufferer and the Suffering Servant. That his sacrifice is worthy of establishing a new covenant also speaks to the greatness of his person, as does the nature of the vindication that God gives to him. Who else is worthy to sit at the right hand of God but one who shares divine status and authority? Thus we turn to the final act that identifies who Jesus is: the resurrection. Here we cover an act that Jesus does not perform, but one where God acts for Jesus, clarifying who he is. In the resurrection, God takes Jesus from the earth up.

Vindication in Resurrection, Ascension, Provision, and Judgment to Come

In the Gospels, at his Jewish examination Jesus develops the significance of his resurrection at the very moment when he is being condemned to the cross (Mark 14:55–64//Matt. 26:59–66//Luke 22:66–71). It appears in Jesus's reply to the question of whether he is the Christ, when he predicts divine vindication for himself. The moment of seeming defeat is the very opportunity for disclosing how God will bring him victory. Upon being asked if he is the Christ, Jesus appeals to Ps. 110:1 and points to God's vindicating him and giving him a seat at God's right hand. One day he will also ride the clouds as Son of Man. All the texts allude to Ps. 110:1 and use the Son of Man title from Dan. 7:13–14. Only Luke does not mention riding the clouds here.

Jesus is claiming that rather than being the defendant before the council, he one day will be their judge, operating from the very side of God.[38] One day they will see the Son of Man seated at the right hand of the Father. Matthew and Luke intensify this remark, noting that "hereafter" (Matthew) or "from now on" (Luke) they will see this exercise of authority. They will not have to wait to see this. The vindication comes soon in what became the empty tomb.

What does Jesus mean by being seated with God besides referring to the fact that he will possess judgment authority one day and gather his elect for their final redemption (the apocalyptic Son of Man texts, esp. Matt. 24:29–31//Mark 13:24–27//Luke 21:25–28; Matt. 25:31–46)? In Acts, this becomes the theme that God has appointed one to be the judge of the living and the dead (Acts 10:42; 17:31). The picture is that all are accountable to Jesus Christ. In John's Gospel this is expressed in the authority of Jesus's words that will

38. The detailed explanation and defense of the historicity of this scene is the burden of Darrell L. Bock, *Blasphemy and Exaltation in Judaism and the Final Examination of Jesus*, WUNT 2/106 (Tübingen: Mohr Siebeck, 1998). The North American edition of this book is *Blasphemy and Exaltation in Judaism: The Charge against Jesus in Mark 14:53–65*, Biblical Studies Library (Grand Rapids: Baker Academic, 2000). The discussion has been updated in my essay "Blasphemy and the Jewish Examination of Jesus," in Bock and Webb, *Key Events in the Life of the Historical Jesus*, 589–667. Among those I interact with on treatments of the question are James D. G. Dunn, *Jesus Remembered* (Grand Rapids: Eerdmans, 2003), 749–54; Adela Yarbro Collins, "The Charge of Blasphemy in Mark 14:64," *JSNT* 26 (2004): 379–401; and Eugene Boring, *Mark* (Louisville: Westminster John Knox, 2006), 413–15. Also providing important detail is one of my articles: Darrell L. Bock, "Jewish Expressions in Mark 14:61–62 and the Authenticity of the Jewish Examination of Jesus," *JSHJ* 1 (2003): 147–59.

be the basis of judgment one day (John 12:48, like Matt. 7:22; John 5:24–29; 11:25–26). The reaction to Jesus is the basis of this judgment in a text that probably is a narrative comment (John 3:18–19). In John's Gospel Jesus's central role is depicted less in his being the judge and more in judgment being determined by how one responds to him.

Clearly Jesus's authority is seen in the role that he has in relationship to final judgment. Is that authority seen anywhere else? Here the promise of provision of the Spirit as evidence that the Christ is present (Luke 3:15–17) in the new era (Luke 24:49; Acts 1:4–8; John 14–16) becomes important. Acts 2 explains the significance of what Jesus declared by pointing to the distribution of the Spirit as a sign of messianic authority and the arrival of divine promise. Jesus's questions about Ps. 110:1 and his initially cryptic claim for vindication at his trial are resolved in Acts 2. Peter's speech refers to Ps. 110:1 (Acts 2:34) as clarifying the resurrection-ascension that Jesus implied through the psalm. Peter's speech in Acts 2 explains that the resurrection is evidence, along with the distribution of the Spirit, that Jesus is Lord and Christ, the bearer of a new era with its long-promised benefits.

In sum, the resurrection leads to Jesus's being given a place at the side of God. His resurrection not only means that there is life after death and a judgment to come, for which all people are accountable to him, but it also points to the identity of the one who brings the promise of life and the Spirit. He is the one qualified to share the very presence of God, distribute the blessing of God, and execute the judgment of God. By taking Jesus from the earth up, God showed who Jesus is, clarified why he was sent, and acted to vindicate Jesus's claims. In the context of a Judaism that held to monotheism, this claim showed a strong identity between Jesus and God, a unity that John's Gospel expresses as a oneness between the Father and Son. It resulted in a confession of Jesus that made him a coregent in heaven, sharing in the divine identity and worthy of confession (John 20:28) and worship. As we have seen throughout this section on Jesus's activity, appreciating who Jesus is does not emerge so much through his verbal claims. The key is to apprehend what his array of acts and the events tied to them tell us about his unique human-divine identity as the Son of Man, who is Son, Messiah, Lord, Servant, and Judge.

Summary of Events and Acts of Jesus

It is the scope and ultimate unity of all of these acts that point to Jesus's uniqueness. Taking most of these categories one by one, we see that parallels with activity by other human divine agents can be found. Moses worked with the creation. Prophets revived the dead. Elijah ended a drought. However, no one attempted or achieved the combination of acts that Jesus performed. The scope of these acts and their theological significance establishes his uniqueness. The directness of his involvement with salvation—in the forgiveness of sins, the sacrificial provision for life, and the giving of the Spirit—tells us that Jesus is more than a human agent commissioned with divine authority. The Gospels argue that the full array of Jesus's acts explains that Jesus the promised Messiah is also the divine Lord. He is the Son of Man who combines humanity and divine prerogatives in unique ways. So Jesus shares not only in divine authority but also in divine personage. Whether one thinks of the Sabbath, the law in general, the changed imagery of the Passover, the temple purging, exorcisms, raising people from the dead, controlling the creation, or forgiving sin—Jesus is doing things that God does and/or exercising authority over things God has set up. The crucifixion is the ground from which God builds his plan of redemption through a uniquely worthy sacrifice. The miracles, and especially the exorcisms, show the scope of Jesus's authority and against whom he is battling to bring victory. The reconfiguring of imagery tied to feasts shows that a new era has come. The work undertaken is greater than that of a religious teacher, ethicist, or prophet. Those categories cannot summarize what Jesus is about or who he is.

Confirming all of this are some sayings that highlight Jesus's unique authority at the hub of divine activity.[39] Numerous texts declare

39. See Robert H. Stein, *The Method and Message of Jesus' Teachings*, rev. ed. (Louisville: Westminster/John Knox, 1994), 122–24, identifying two categories of

the authority that Jesus has to judge and acknowledge others before God (Matt. 10:32–33; Mark 8:34–38; Matt. 10:40//Mark 9:37) or that blessing comes from not being offended at him (Matt. 11:6). The apocalyptic Son of Man sayings fit here as well. Jesus stands at the center of divine blessing in several "I" sayings that show his authority (Matt. 11:28, over rest; 5:17, over law; Mark 2:17, over forgiveness; Luke 19:10, over the lost; 12:49, to bring fire). He is greater than Abraham (John 8:58), than Jacob (John 4:12–14), than Solomon and Jonah (Matt. 12:38–42//Luke 11:29–32). He is greater even than the temple (Matt. 12:6). Several sayings point to his having come or having been sent from heaven (Matt. 5:17; 10:34–35, 40; 11:19; 15:24; Mark 9:37; Luke 4:18, 43; 5:32; 9:48; 10:16; 12:49; 19:10; John 5:23–24, 30, 37, 43; 6:29, 38, 39, 42, 44, 57; 7:29; 8:16, 18, 26, 29, 42; 9:4, 39; 10:10, 36; 11:42; 12:44–45, 49; 13:20; 14:24; 15:21; 16:5; 17:3, 8, 18, 21, 23, 25).[40] The parable of the wicked tenants pictures Jesus as the sent Son (Mark 12:1–12//Matt. 21:33–46//Luke 20:9–19). In sum, Jesus is unique as the revelator of God, standing in the middle of divine deliverance.

The resurrection-ascension is the ultimate vindication of these claims. The judgment to come is the ultimate proof that Jesus possesses absolute authority. However, in the current era, it is the provision of the Spirit as the enabler of his children that points to this uniquely authoritative Jesus. His seated position at the side of God shows that he shares completely in divinity. He is the one who is both Lord and Christ. In an ultimate way, the resurrection takes Jesus from the earth up, adjudicating the dispute between Jesus and the Jewish

---

sayings here: (1) the totalitarian claims of Jesus; and (2) Jesus's comparing himself with OT saints. This paragraph reflects these sections.

40. The burden of what these texts teach in terms of Jesus's self-understanding as seen in his mission texts is treated by Simon Gathercole, *The Preexistent Son: Recovering the Christologies of Matthew, Mark and Luke* (Grand Rapids: Eerdmans, 2006). In tracing this theme, Gathercole is arguing that, in their portrayal of Jesus's self-understanding, the Christologies of the Synoptic Gospels are not as distinct from John as some contend. What this chapter has tried to show is that when one adds to this the significance of Jesus's acts, especially those we see in the Synoptics, the distance shrinks even more, so that the difference becomes more one of rhetorical strategy versus substance. The Synoptics tell the story more from the earth up, while John tells it from heaven down. Each narrative takes one to the same conclusion about the uniqueness of Jesus.

leaders with a divine vote of action. From the very side of God, Jesus has brought the promised new era of God and with it a new community filled with new promise.

What does this new community of the new era look like? To that question we now turn.

6

Jesus's Community of the New Era: The Calling of Those Who Respond

Living as a Child Who Reflects and Honors the Father

The Gospels are somewhat enigmatic when it comes to defining the origins of the new community that Jesus's ministry forged. On the one hand, Jesus preached to Israel and called for reform in fulfillment of the arrival of the new era. His actions, as well as those of the Baptist, appear to call for repentance and a renewed walk with God in line with long-established hopes. John and Jesus both preached to Israel about Israel's hope. The call to reform was an invitation to step into a long-hoped-for kingdom promise. Nothing about this message required that a distinct group apart from Israel be formed.

The reaction that Jesus received drove events in a fresh direction. The rejection and opposition he experienced prevented his followers from fully assimilating into the Jewish community. Those who responded to Jesus were somewhat distinct, despite their message of continuity. Jesus did little to discourage this as he formed his own group of followers and trained them in ways reminiscent of the way rabbis functioned, with the important exception of his calling them to be his students rather than the students coming to him. At this level, Jesus looks like a specially endowed "charismatic" figure whose authority and claim of a special relationship to God produced a following. This led to the emergence of a new social group within Judaism.[1]

So Jesus called out a special group of followers and formed the most important members into a band of twelve to lead this new community. They were to depict the renewal of the nation in a fresh teaching and leadership structure and call people to the kingdom path of renewal and participation in the promise Jesus was preaching. The term "church" (ἐκκλησία), the name eventually assigned to this group, is rarely used in the Gospels, appearing only three times (Matt. 16:18; 18:17 [2×]). The rarity of the term there reflects the ambiguity of how the church arose as a separate entity, leaving the impression that the emergence of this new and distinct entity took some time to surface. Its basic meaning of "assembly" could be the meaning in

1. The term "charismatic" is used here in a technical sociological sense of an appealing, publicly powerful leader figure. Some like to argue that Jesus was such a figure, with no "institutional" goals. In other words, he had no interest in forming a new community or structure. This often is summarized in the view that Jesus came to reform Israel, but what came instead was a church that he never intended to create. Such a dichotomy between Jesus as a charismatic figure and as an institutional founder is rightly challenged by John Meier, "Dividing Lines in Jesus Research Today: Through Dialectical Negation to a Positive Sketch," *Interpretation* 50 (1996): 366–68. Those who argue for Jesus as charismatic but not an institutional founder argue that Jesus, having apocalyptic goals, would not be interested in founding a new community when the nearness of the end is so emphasized. However, Meier correctly observes that the Qumran community was apocalyptic in its worldview and yet formed an entirely restructured community as they anticipated the arrival of the end. The evidence that Meier gives for Jesus's institutional concerns include his forming an inner group of disciples, the circle of the Twelve; the role of baptism among his followers; and subsequently the formulation of a prayer for his disciples and the institution of a unique symbolic fellowship meal. All of these elements are multiply attested in the Gospel tradition. Jesus's selection of the Twelve also points in the direction that he sought to form a community of his own making, even while arguing that this group was in continuity with the hope of the Hebrew Scripture. The question of whether the church that emerged was always designed to be a distinct entity is more complicated. The church argued that in the promise tied to Jesus were found the promises of old. What certainly helped to make the church a distinct entity was the rejection by most of official Judaism. That story is one of the burdens of the book of Acts. For details on the purposes of Acts, see Darrell L. Bock, *A Theology of Luke and Acts: God's Promised Program, Realized for All Nations* (Grand Rapids: Zondervan, 2012).

these Gospel passages, although Jesus's reference to "my" assembly in Matt. 16 makes clear that he does have in mind something fresh and distinct from what currently exists. Thus there is an inherent complexity in the way the presentation of Jesus in Scripture handles this question of community.

As important as its structure are the community's character and calling. In fact, Jesus spends much more time here than on questions of the community's form and structure. Those who ally themselves to Jesus and the community built around him and his teaching are called to take on a certain lifestyle in relationship to the world, others, and life. Belonging to this theme are Jesus's teaching on discipleship and discussion of ethical values as a means of testimony to God. So in this section we consider the forming of community in the call to discipleship and the calling of that community in terms of Jesus's ethical teaching and ministries of service and mission. This section will alternate between themes tied to the formation and structure of a new community and its ethical commitments.

Response to Grace: Repentance and Faith

We have examined repentance and faith already in the discussion on kingdom. However, since this response forms the basis of the relationship from which Jesus builds and defines his own mission, it needs to be examined in further detail.

The calling of Levi/Matthew and the controversial relationships with outsiders it represented led Jesus to make a mission statement that he, like a physician, had come to call the sick—that is, sinners (Matt. 9:10–13//Mark 2:15–17). In commenting on this same scene, Luke adds that the calling is to repentance (Luke 5:32). Similar in thrust is a text unique to Matthew (4:17), where the summary of Jesus's message is "Repent, for the kingdom of heaven is at hand." Those who would enter the kingdom of God must appreciate their need for his direction and rule in their lives. They must acknowledge their need for God and for coming to him on his terms. Luke, in a passage unique to his Gospel (13:1–5), makes the same point in discussing fatal tragedy. Rather than discussing whether tragedy is the result of a worse type of sin, Jesus warns that without repentance, his audience will likewise perish. At the base of this repentance and turning to God is a humility that expresses itself in a trust that only God can supply what one needs for salvation. This open and dependent attitude for God is the avenue for responsiveness to God. One who trusts and humbly senses a need for what another must supply is responsive to the one doing the gifting.

Additional evidence of Luke's emphasis on this theme is Luke 15:7, 10, which notes how heaven rejoices when a sinner repents, as an explanation for why Jesus associates with sinners. A final uniquely Lukan text (24:47) highlights Jesus's commissioning of a message for the newly emerging community: "repentance for the forgiveness of sins will be preached in his name to all nations, beginning at Jerusalem" (NIV). This message is a realization of teaching expressed in the OT (Luke 24:44–47).

Failure to repent will lead to judgment (Matt. 11:20//Luke 10:13; Matt. 12:41//Luke 11:32). Thus this repentance theme is multiply attested. It expresses the response from the standpoint of its starting point. To come to Jesus is to have a change of perspective about God and a change of direction from the path that one previously was traveling. To come to Jesus as to a physician is like coming to him for healing from a spiritual disease. It permits the doctor to prescribe the medicine and set the direction of spiritual care.

A second key term of response is "faith," which most often appears in the Gospels as a response and expectation that God can act, often through Jesus. Here we find faith affirmed in the centurion (Matt. 8:10, 13//Luke 7:9), the friends of the paralytic (Matt. 9:2// Mark 2:5//Luke 5:20), the woman with the hemorrhage (Matt. 9:22// Mark 5:34, 36//Luke 8:48), the healing of the boy with the unclean spirit (Mark 9:23–24), the healing of two blind men (Matt. 9:28–29, similar to the commendation of Bartimaeus in Mark 10:52//Luke 18:42), the Gentile woman (Matt. 15:28, where the Markan parallel does not mention faith), the parents of the girl who has died (Luke 8:50), and the sinful woman (Luke 7:50). Jesus exhorts the disciples to have faith in their prayers and life (Matt. 17:20//Luke 17:5–6; Matt. 21:21–22//Mark 11:22–24; Luke 22:32; discourse not using the term "faith" but describing such trust: Matt. 6:25–33, like Luke 12:22–34).

In the Gospels the term "faith" is rarely used as a technical term for entry into the community. Faith reflects an attitude that God honors with his gracious response involving acts of deliverance through Jesus. In this way the term pictures the more technical theological usage that the attitude came to have in the early church.

However, more technical uses of "faith" as the response to Jesus's message do appear. In Matt. 18:6, the verb is used to summarize the defining characteristic of children of God as "little ones who believe" (//Mark 9:42). In addition, in Mark 1:15, it is used as a summary term of response to Jesus's call to believe the gospel of the kingdom, where both "repent" and "believe" appear. This passage is significant since it points to how repentance and faith are related. Repentance is the change of mind that starts the transition to embracing what God has done. Faith is the trust where it ends up. In the humility it takes to turn are the seeds for the faith that believes and trusts. In Matt. 27:42 the verb is used ironically by taunters who say they will believe if Jesus comes down from the cross (//Mark 15:32). The idea of believing also is a summary term for what Satan prevents in the Lukan version of the parable of the seed (Luke 8:12; a reference to short-lived faith is present in 8:13). Jesus rebukes the two traveling to Emmaus for their lack of belief (Luke 24:25).

In John's Gospel, the noun "faith" is not used. However, it does show up in its verbal form as the summary response term. In fact, John's use of the act of believing parallels the Epistles' use of the term "faith" as a summary term (John 1:7, 12; 2:11, 23; 3:12, 15, 16, 18, 36; 4:39; 5:24, 46; 6:29, 35, 40, 47, 69; 7:31, 38; 8:24, 31, short-lived faith; 9:38; 10:25–26, 42; 11:25–27, 48; 12:11, 36, 42, 44, 46; 14:1, 10–12; 16:27, 30–31; 17:8, 20–21; 19:35; 20:8, 25, 29, 31). No text highlights the importance of faith and its dynamic ongoing character more than John 6:60–68, where Peter confesses for the disciples that they will not walk away from Jesus, because he has the words of life. The concept of abiding in Jesus's word has its roots in a response like this (John 15:1–11). Here is a response that looks at reception in terms of where it ends up. It trusts in God and his work through Jesus. As such, the term is not static, merely a response in a single moment. Instead, it is turning and embracing God in a faith that trusts him for what is offered through Jesus. Faith is not about just one moment, though it starts there; it is about an orientation toward God as one who believes him.

Calling Disciples and the Twelve

Call to and Commitment of Discipleship

Seven texts are prominent when it comes to picturing the calling of disciples. When Jesus walks by some fishermen cleaning their nets, they drop what they are doing and leave everything behind to follow him (Mark 1:16–20//Matt. 4:18–22). The call here is to become "fishers" of people. Similar is a scene that confirms this call with the miraculous catch of fish (Luke 5:1–11). The additional element here is the surfacing of Peter's exemplary attitude whereby he obeys Jesus in casting the nets despite the seeming futility of the instruction. Peter confesses his sinfulness, a humility that Jesus can work with because Peter is responsive to him. Peter thought that his sin meant he could not be with one whom he sensed was walking with God, but Jesus knew that by Peter's recognizing his sinful status and need for God, Peter was exactly the kind of person God can minister to and bring into the community.

The call of Levi shows Jesus reaching out to the "rejected" of society (Matt. 9:9–13//Mark 2:13–17//Luke 5:27–32). We previously noted the mission statement about Jesus's call to sinners that this event produced. Tax collectors were less than respected because they were seen as cooperating with the Romans. Jesus's call to them showed that God's call was for anyone who was willing to respond.

There is another set of discipleship-call texts, in which the priority of putting this response above everything else, including the family requirement to bury a father, shows it to be the single most important decision one makes (Matt. 8:19–22//Luke 9:57–62). Similar in force are texts that state how Jesus will divide families because some will embrace him and others will not (Matt. 10:34–39//Luke 12:49–53).

Luke 14:25–35 makes clear to the multitudes that the cost of discipleship must be counted. Jesus wanted the crowds to know what the walk entailed before they started into it. They are to count the cost and be prepared for the effort that lies ahead in walking down the path of following Jesus amid opposition. Still, it is better to pursue peace with a more powerful God than to oppose him.

Kingdom parables pointing to the value of being in the kingdom make the same point while picturing a related concept (Matt. 13:44–46). Jesus's point is clear: the kingdom is so precious and valuable that it is worth selling everything to obtain. Appreciating all that the kingdom offers is what makes it worth the sacrifice.

The Twelve

The formation of the Twelve also shows Jesus's intent to build a community around people whom he expects one day to lead his new movement (Matt. 10:2–4//Mark 3:16–19//Luke 6:13–16).[2] It is these twelve whom he sends out into mission to call Israel to the kingdom and repentance. Jesus gives them ability to illustrate the coming of God's rule with miraculous authority (Matt. 10:1–15//Luke 9:1–6). After hearing Peter's messianic confession (Matt. 16:13–20), Jesus tells the leader of these twelve that he will build his church. To the Twelve Jesus promises a kingdom and the right to sit over the twelve tribes of Israel (Luke 22:29–30//Matt. 19:28). Jesus is intentionally restructuring the people of God around a community that he forms. Interestingly, he does not count himself as one of the Twelve, for he stands distinct and above them in authority.

Jesus shows intentionality in his forming of the Twelve to be his new community. He is forming a community grounded in humble dedication to God, expressing a renewal and realization of Israel's hope. The choice of the Twelve shows that Jesus consciously seeks to parallel Israel and make a claim on Israel. That the Twelve will judge Israel shows how the authority of promise now resides in this newly formed group. This kind of expectation also points to a figure of unique authority who can make a claim over the nation.

2. For a full development of this theme and a defense of its fundamental historicity, see Scot McKnight, "Jesus and the Twelve," *Bulletin for Biblical Research* 11 (2001): 203–31; and the chapter with the same title in *Key Events in the Life of the Historical Jesus: A Collaborative Exploration of Context and Coherence*, ed. Darrell L. Bock and Robert L. Webb (Tübingen: Mohr Siebeck, 2009), 181–214.

The mission of the Twelve is to call others into this new relationship, which connects to Israel's hope but is distinct from some current structures in Israel. The emphasis and priorities of those who see their need for God and his rule as Jesus represents it will be different from those of current Judaism, with its focus on Jewish identity markers tied to the law. This leads us into the theme of discipleship and the inherent reaction that such a calling evokes from the community needing reform, the community out of which the new group emerged.

The All-Encompassing Character of Discipleship

On Disciples

We previously identified seven texts in which a calling to follow Jesus takes place.[3] They highlight how the call to mission led the disciples immediately to leave their previous vocational tasks and accompany Jesus. A prominent theme in all the Gospels is discipleship and referring to those who embrace Jesus as disciples. The noun "disciple" (μαθητής) appears frequently in each Gospel and refers to a "learner." It appears 72 times in Matthew, 46 times in Mark, 37 times in Luke, and 78 times in John. The term is not used again in the NT outside of the book of Acts. Hence this is a term associated with Jesus's ministry.

Total Commitment

Discipleship involves a total commitment. All other relationships take a backseat to it, including caring for one's parents in death, a category that Jesus selects because it was considered to be one of the highest familial duties (Luke 9:59//Matt. 8:21–22). No one pursuing discipleship is to pause to inform family, an image that stands in contrast to Elijah's calling of Elisha (Luke 9:61–62; cf. 1 Kings

3. The seven calling texts are as follows: two accounts of the call to the four fishermen, plus the call of Levi, the miraculous catch of fish, the text on dividing families, the parables showing the value of the kingdom, and the urgent call to count the cost of discipleship. For this section, see Richard N. Longenecker, ed., *Patterns of Discipleship in the New Testament*, McMaster New Testament Studies (Grand Rapids: Eerdmans, 1996), 1–97.

19:19–21). In fact, the choice to follow Jesus could well split families (Matt. 10:34–39//Luke 12:49–53).

Discipleship involves a struggle to grasp all that it requires, and so progress can be difficult. One of the unique elements in Mark's Gospel is how it portrays the disciples as stumbling and bumbling their way through their walk with Jesus during his lifetime. Luke 9 also portrays many missteps, but Jesus treats the disciples with patience because they desire to follow him. Discipleship does not come easy. Failure sometimes takes place, but the goal is to be on a trajectory that grows in faithfulness.

Discipleship is to be entered into with forethought lest one embarrassingly not complete the assignment (Luke 14:25–35). However, it also should be entered into with an awareness that one is not stronger than God. So one should not oppose him. Thus, discipleship is to come first, ahead of all other allegiances and relationships, including to one's own life (Matt. 10:37//Luke 14:26; Matt. 16:25//Mark 8:35//Luke 9:24; Luke 14:33).

Suffering and Rejection

Discipleship also entails suffering, taking up the cross, which Luke alone notes is taken up "daily" (Matt. 16:24//Mark 8:34//Luke 9:23). It means an unsettled life (Matt. 8:19–20//Luke 9:57–58). For Luke, the disciple will appreciate that separation from the world means a different attitude toward possessions (Luke 12:13–21; 16:10–13; Matt. 6:24). So the disciple lives in a tension between engaging the world with the gospel while serving in it to show God's love and grace and a lifestyle that is not too attached to the world, living in ways distinct from the world's values. Often summarized as being in the world but not of the world, the point is that a different way of living shows how God's ways are distinct from the kind of self-interest that often comes with the way of the world.

For John's Gospel, discipleship means facing rejection from the Jews and a separation from the world (John 9:22; 12:42; 16:2; 17:14–16). In John's Gospel, believing in Jesus is central to defining who a follower of Jesus is. To be a disciple is to know the Father and the Son (John 6:69; 17:3). In fact, for John the definition of eternal life is to know the Father and the Son. It is a life of quality, not just of duration. It means being a member of Jesus's personal flock, those who recognize his voice (John 10:7–18). The disciple bears fruit (15:1–7), loves (15:12–13), and serves (13:14–16).

The Disciple's Character: Love, Grace, Forgiveness, Mercy, and Service

The character of the disciple also is a topic of concern. Love is a primary characteristic. The theme of the disciple's love shows up in the Synoptics (Matt. 22:34–40//Mark 12:28–31, like Luke 10:25–28). One is to love God fully and one's neighbor. Jesus calls such love the essence of what the kingdom is about when he declares that understanding this leaves one not far from the kingdom.

Forgiveness also is a characteristic of the disciple, as the Lord's Prayer points out, and as is dramatically demonstrated in a parable unique to Matthew (18:21–35). Disciples forgive because they have experienced forgiveness. They are to show grace even to those outside the faith and to enemies because they themselves have experienced grace and mercy (Matt. 5:44–45//Luke 6:35–36).

Leadership is to be exercised not in acts of power, as is done among the Gentiles, but in service (Matt. 20:25–28//Mark 10:42–45//Luke 22:24–27). The disciple also is called to mission (Matt. 5:14–16; 28:18–20; Luke 24:47). Service is the expression of love, care, mercy, and grace. Disciples are to be known for their love (John 13:34–35). It shows that their pedigree can be traced back to God. Jesus issues this command just after he has washed the disciples' feet, thus pointing to the link between love and service.

Many of the parables pick up themes tied to discipleship and emphasize that disciples must do the following:

- heed what Jesus teaches (house on the rock, Matt. 7:24–27//Luke 6:47–49)
- forgive (two debtors, Luke 7:41–44; unlike the unforgiving servant, Matt. 18:23–35)
- respond to the word (the sower, Mark 4:1–20//Matt. 13:1–23//Luke 8:4–15)

- love one's neighbor (good Samaritan, Luke 10:29–37)
- pray (bold neighbor, Luke 11:5–8; nagging widow, Luke 18:1–8)
- be generous (rich fool, Luke 12:13–21; rich man and Lazarus, Luke 16:19–31)
- be accountable to God and alert to him until Christ returns (watchful servant, Luke 12:35–48; ten virgins, Matt. 25:1–13; pounds/talents, Luke 19:11–27, like Matt. 25:14–30; fig tree, Luke 21:29–33)
- be humble (seats at the banquet, Luke 14:7–14; Pharisee and tax collector, Luke 18:9–14)
- be totally committed to God (tower and warring king, Luke 14:25–33)
- serve as a matter of duty (uncommended servant, Luke 17:7–10)
- be useful (salt, Matt. 5:13, like Luke 14:34–35; also, with the image of light, Luke 11:33–34)

Through these parables Jesus points to the array of traits that make up the effective disciple. Jesus was concerned that those who follow him be prepared for the task and appreciate what a calling to walk in God's way involves. These themes also are multiply attested, appearing at all levels of the Gospel tradition. Much of Jesus's practical instruction and ethical emphasis shows up in discourses on discipleship or in parabolic teaching. We will return to some of these themes tied to expressed righteousness when we consider how Jesus calls on his followers to relate to the world.

The Role of Parables

The parables, so prominent in discipleship teaching, were also a veiled form of teaching that reflected a judgment on those who did not wish to embrace Jesus (Matt. 13:10–17//Mark 4:10–12//Luke 8:9–10). They were mysteries through which the kingdom and the calling were revealed.[4]

4. Using parables is one of the more prominent aspects of Jesus's teaching. We simply summarize its contribution to show the breadth of its usage; a full discussion

The parables cover far more than issues of discipleship and spiritual life. They can be sorted into the following eighteen themes:

- now is the new day of salvation (Matt. 9:14–17//Mark 2:18–22//Luke 5:33–38; Mark 4:21–25//Luke 8:16)
- the call to pay attention to the light (Matt. 6:22–23//Luke 11:34–36)
- the invitation to the banquet (Matt. 22:1–10; Luke 14:15–24)
- the mercy of God for sinners and lost disciples (sinners: Luke 7:41–43; 15:11–32; 18:9–14; disciples: Matt. 18:10–14)
- the great assurance of access to God (Luke 11:5–8; 18:1–8)
- the kingdom and its growth (Matt. 13:31–33//Luke 13:18–21)
- the imminence of catastrophe or judgment (Matt. 25:31–46; Luke 12:16–21, 49–53; Matt. 10:34–36//Luke 12:51–53; 13:6–9)
- it may be too late (Luke 13:6–9; 14:15–24//Matt. 22:1–14)
- the need to listen to and obey Jesus (Luke 6:47–49//Matt. 7:24–27; Luke 11:24–26//Matt. 12:43–45; Luke 12:58–59)
- accountability as a matter of faithful serving (Luke 16:1–9; 17:7–10; Matt. 25:14–30//Luke 19:12–27; Matt. 21:28–32)
- care for the poor and warnings about wealth (Luke 12:13–21; 16:19–31)
- the call to love (Luke 10:25–37)
- the call not to worry (Matt. 6:25–34//Luke 12:22–32)
- the way is narrow (Matt. 7:13–14, like Luke 13:23–24)
- the return (Matt. 24:45–51; Luke 12:35–40)
- the kingdom in general (Matt. 13//Mark 4//Luke 8:4–15; Luke 13:19–21)
- the equality of grace (Matt. 20:1–16)

---

would call for a full volume. For more detail, see Klyne Snodgrass, *Stories with Intent: A Comprehensive Guide to the Parables of Jesus* (Grand Rapids: Eerdmans, 2008); Craig Blomberg, *Interpreting the Parables* (Downers Grove, IL: InterVarsity, 1991); Simon Kistemaker, *The Parables of Jesus* (Grand Rapids: Baker, 1980); Joachim Jeremias, *The Parables of Jesus*, trans. S. H. Hooke, rev. ed., New Testament Library (Philadelphia: Westminster, 1963).

- the rejection and exaltation of the Son in the face of wicked tenants (Matt. 21:33–46//Mark 12:1–12//Luke 20:9–19)

The use of these instructional stories was one of the most basic elements of Jesus's teaching. The bulk of the parables treat themes tied to describing the kingdom, the return and its associated judgment, or the behavior of disciples. Issues of responding to the kingdom and the accountability for that response are also frequent. The parables are designed to make us pause and reimage the way we think about and respond to God. They teach not with abstract words but with images that push us to see the world and our role in it differently.

Community: Israel, Expansion to Gentiles, and Worship

Israel

One of the oddities for a modern reader of the Gospels is how focused Jesus's mission was on Israel. However, it is too often forgotten that Jesus's program was a realization of promises originally made to that nation. It was the program of the God of Abraham, Isaac, and Jacob. Nothing in Jesus's activity indicates that he diverted from these roots in terms of the focus of his own program, although there also are hints that Jesus foresaw a day when his effort would reach out to the nations.[5]

Several texts point to Jesus's concern for Israel, with the concentration of such texts tied to Jesus's remarks appearing in Matthew's

5. Recent approaches to Jesus have emphasized how in line with Israel and its hopes this story was. Both G. B. Caird (*New Testament Theology*, compiled and ed. L. D. Hurst [Oxford: Clarendon, 1994], 350–66) and N. T. Wright (*Jesus and the Victory of God* [Minneapolis: Fortress, 1996]) see this as the central, defining feature of Jesus's message. In the offer of the kingdom, Jesus declares the end of Israel's spiritual exile. For an assessment of Wright's approach, see Carey C. Newman, ed., *Jesus and the Restoration of Israel: A Critical Assessment of N. T. Wright's "Jesus and the Victory of God"* (Downers Grove, IL: InterVarsity, 1999). A classic work discussing these themes is Joachim Jeremias, *Jesus' Promise to the Nations*, trans. S. H. Hooke, rev. ed. (Philadelphia: Fortress, 1982). It is the distinctive feature of the third quest for the historical Jesus to focus on understanding Jesus out of his Jewish context and appreciating the point of his ministry to Israel.

Gospel.[6] In the mission of the disciples, Jesus sends them out only to "the lost sheep . . . of Israel," specifically excluding a mission to Gentiles or to Samaria (Matt. 10:5–6). He sees this mission to Israelite towns as continuing until the Son of Man comes (Matt. 10:23). This verse, often debated, means that ministry to Israel is to continue until the Son of Man returns. When confronted by a Gentile, Jesus specifically says that he "was sent only to the lost sheep of the house of Israel" (Matt. 15:24; interestingly, Mark lacks this specific response). Ironically, Matthew relates how some perceptive Gentiles respond to the presence of Jesus, showing that their inclusion is not prohibited by this initial focus on Israel: Magi (Matt. 2), centurion (Matt. 8:5–13 [//Luke 7:1–10]), Syrophoenician woman (Matt. 15:21–28), centurion (Matt. 27:54 [//Mark 15:39//Luke 23:47]). The success of Jesus's ministry means that the God of Israel receives the glory (Matt. 15:31).

Eschatologically, Israel is still in view, as one day the twelve apostles will judge the twelve tribes of Israel (Matt. 19:28//Luke 22:30). Israel has a desolate house until its people say, "Blessed is he who comes in the name of the Lord" (Matt. 23:37–39//Luke 13:34–35). So Israel is accountable for its rejection of Jesus, but the hope is for a day when faith will come and the Messiah will be embraced.

Narrative remarks point to this focus as well. The citation of Mic. 5:2 leads to a description in Matt. 2:6 of Jesus as one who will govern God's people Israel. The taunting on the cross causes some to joke about Jesus as "King of Israel" (Matt. 27:42; Mark 15:32). The births of John and of Jesus lead to a mission for Israel in line with covenant and prophetic hope (Luke 1:16, 54, 68). Simeon's welcome to Jesus is that of a faithful Jew who was looking for "the consolation of Israel" (Luke 2:25). According to Simeon, Jesus comes as "glory for your people Israel" and one who will be "set for the fall and rising of many in Israel" (Luke 2:32 CEB; 2:34). The two disciples on the road to Emmaus had hoped that Jesus would be "the one to redeem Israel" (Luke 24:21). In John's Gospel, the witness of John the Baptist

6. Mark does not even raise this theme in any detail, probably because of his Gentile audience. With the letter *J* indicating that Jesus is speaking, see seven relevant texts in Matthew (2:6; 10:6 [J], 23 [J]; 15:24 [J], 31; 19:28 [J]; 27:42); and seven such in Luke, but most of his texts are in narrative remarks (1:54, 68; 2:25, 32, 34; 22:30 [J] [//Matt. 19:28]; 24:21).

is that Jesus received the confirmation of heaven at the baptism "that he might be revealed to Israel" (John 1:31). Both Nathanael and the crowds that greet Jesus's entry to Jerusalem hail him as "King of Israel" (John 1:49; 12:13). As previously noted, Jesus's forming of the Twelve points to an intent to reform Israel and rule over Israel.

Jesus's pronouncement of judgment on the nation also shows his national concern. Here the Olivet Discourse is prominent (Matt. 24//Mark 13//Luke 21), but so are earlier remarks about Israel or Jerusalem's coming fate and the image of the withered fig tree (Luke 13:6–9, 34–35; 19:41–44; 23:27–31). Some of these texts hold out hope that this judgment is not final, that one day the "times of the Gentiles" will be done. As was just noted, Israel's house is desolate until they cry out, "Blessed is the one who comes in the name of the Lord" (Luke 21:24; 13:35). So much of Jesus's concern for Israel is seen also in how he handled issues of law and purity (treated earlier in this book). His goal was to instruct and reform Israel in its walk with the God of promise. The condition of Israel and the arrival of the new era called for such reform, as John the Baptist's ministry also suggested.

Expansion to Gentiles

However, it would be wrong to suggest that the portrait of Jesus in the Gospels ignored the potential inclusion of the nations in Jesus's mission.[7] Three of his more prominent miracles involved Gentiles: the centurion (Matt. 8:5–13//Luke 7:1–10), the Gentile woman's daughter (Mark 7:24–30//Matt. 15:21–28), and the Gadarene demoniac (probably Gentile, since this Decapolis area was predominantly Gentile and pigs are involved in the miracle; Mark 5:1–20//Matt. 8:28–34// Luke 8:26–39). Even though Jesus's initial response to the Gentile woman asking him to heal her daughter is a reply about the exclusive focus of his call, he moves to honor her request. Jesus also drew from

7. There is another class of texts that show how Jesus used the Gentiles as a negative example of how the world operates. In these passages the Gentiles become the measure of how not to act (Matt. 5:47; Matt. 6:32//Luke 12:30; Matt. 20:25//Mark 10:42; Luke 22:25). The tone of these texts shows how deeply Jewish Jesus is in his teaching perspective.

Gentile areas, as the summaries of the location of his work and the sources of the crowds before the Sermon on the Mount make clear (Matt. 4:13–15, 24–25). People come from places like the Decapolis and Syria. Jesus's ministry of bringing justice and hope to the nations is in line with the call of the Servant and is expressed in a narrative note in Matt. 12:18–21. Luke also makes this point. In the synagogue sermon in Luke 4:25–27, Jesus suggests that Israel's lack of response will produce a time like that of Elijah and Elisha, when blessing came only to Gentiles, a remark that sparks the Jewish audience's anger.[8] In addition, the work of John the Baptist and the one who comes after him represent the time when "all flesh shall see the salvation of God" (Luke 3:6).

Other texts explicitly have Jesus teaching that those included in the banquet at the end will involve many coming from north, south, east, and west, but some of Israel will be excluded. That this theme shows up in Matt. 8:11–12 is interesting given Matthew's concern for the outreach to Israel (also in Luke 13:28–29). John 4 and 12 present Jesus in dialogues with Samaritans and Greeks, while Luke 9:51–56 has Jesus sending a mission into Samaria. Luke 17:11–19 has Jesus commending the faith of a Samaritan, fitting the multiple appeals to this idea in Matthew. These hints about Gentiles are a multiply attested theme in the Gospels. In Mark 11:17, the temple is to be "a house of prayer for all the nations," probably looking to a day in the future when the nations will stream to Jerusalem to pray and worship (citing Isa. 56:7; rooted in Gen. 12:1–3, see also Isa. 2:2–4; 19:23–25; 42:6; 49:6; 66:19–20; Mic. 4:1–2; Zech. 14:16).[9] Jesus explicitly mentions how the mission of the disciples involves going out into all the world (Matt. 24:14//Mark 13:10; Matt. 26:13//Mark 14:9). The vineyard, lacking fruit from Israel, will be given to another nation bearing fruit (Matt. 21:33–46//Mark 12:1–10//Luke 20:9–19). Here "nation" includes Jews and Gentiles, since the Twelve would be seen as a remnant from Israel. At the end of his ministry, Jesus gives commissions to reach out to all the nations (Matt. 28:18–20; Luke 24:44–47; Acts 1:8).

8. This theme extends to Acts, where 20:21–22 shows the same reaction meeting Paul when he speaks of Gentile inclusion in God's blessing.

9. For this theme, see Jeremias, *Jesus' Promise to the Nations*, 57–73.

The book of Acts describes the gospel being preached to all the nations, a theme running so counter to the focus of Jesus's own earthly ministry. This outreach to all took time to sink in for the disciples. However, nothing in Jesus's ministry, even as it focused on Israel, precluded the inclusion of the nations. In fact, a look at how the relationship of Jew and Gentile plays itself out underscores what Paul said later about the gospel being "to the Jew first and also to the Greek" (Rom. 1:16).

All of this emphasis is in line with the prophetic hope, except that Jesus's teaching lacks any notes of retribution against the nations as such. As we will see, the vindication that God brings in judgment will be directed at the wicked, whoever they may be. God will move to gather the righteous who have welcomed Jesus and those associated with him (Matt. 25:31–46). The kingdom's authority and reach will extend out over the entire world (Matt. 13:37–43). The new community will be made up of Jews and Gentiles, reconciled to God and to each other, a theme vividly picked up in Eph. 2:11–22. When one considers the contentious history of Jews and Gentiles as depicted vividly in the Maccabean War (1 Macc. 1–2), then this move truly does represent bringing together people who have long been at odds.[10]

Worship

When it comes to religious practice and worship, Jesus also is at points very Jewish. He goes to the synagogue and ministers (Luke 4:16–30//Matt. 13:53–58//Mark 6:1–6; Matt. 12:9–14//Mark 3:1–6//Luke 6:6–11; Luke 13:10–17). He sends a healed leper to the priest in obedience to the law (Mark 1:40–45//Matt. 8:2–4//Luke 5:12–16). He teaches in the temple courts and is concerned for the well-being of the temple, as the cleansing incident shows. In this way, he is typically Jewish.

10. From the perspective of pious Jews, 1 Macc. 1–2 vividly depicts how threatened they felt by the Gentile presence because of idolatry and past efforts to wipe out Jewish practice. Understanding this background is crucial to appreciating why Gentile inclusion was revolutionary. It also helps to explain why maintaining Jewish distinctives and seeking to keep the law as a sign of faithfulness were so important to many Jews.

However, other acts show a conscious effort by Jesus to be distinct. He is not particularly sensitive to some issues of purity tied to hand washing or to the touching of lepers or the dead (Luke 7:11–17; 11:37–41; Mark 7:1–23//Matt. 15:1–20). He is willing to create a prayer that is distinct for his disciples (Luke 11:1–4). His remarks at the Last Supper lead to the institution of a meal of remembrance and affirmation by his disciples.

Interestingly, Jesus says nothing about the form of worship. What he calls for is integrity in worship: the one who approaches the altar should do so without having anything against a brother or sister (Matt. 5:21–26), and those who tithe should also remember justice, love, mercy, and faith (Matt. 23:23–24, like Luke 11:42–43). Worship is to be "in spirit and truth" (John 4:24). Matthew and Luke, especially Luke, have Jesus praying regularly and encouraging prayer as well as acts of charity (Luke 3:21; 11:1–13; Matt. 6:1–18; 7:7–11). The vulnerable position of those whom he seeks to serve is pictured in the image of the flock or the picture of lost sheep (Matt. 9:35–38; 10:6; 15:24; Mark 14:27; Luke 12:32; 15:3–7). This is why the community needs to hear the voice of the shepherd sent from God (John 10:1–18).

Clearly, the community that Jesus forms is to be in healthy, dependent communion with God, living a life of righteous character, which brings us to the next topic concerning community. Righteousness is a goal within the love for God and neighbor: disciples are to be perfect as the Father is perfect (Matt. 5:48; 13:43; 25:46). Jesus is about calling sinners to be made into the righteous (Matt. 9:13//Mark 2:17//Luke 5:32).

The Character of the Disciple in the Relationship to the World

Here we consider five major areas: love and mercy, righteous integrity, possessions and the world, suffering, and service-mission. Earlier we introduced this theme while examining the character of the disciple. Here we expand that introductory look by considering how that character engages with the world.

Love and Mercy

Jesus's command to love and have mercy serves as the basis for his ethical call. Several texts make this point. The most dramatic text is Mark 12:28–34//Matt. 22:35–40 (like Luke 10:25–28). Here a question about the primary commandment invokes the Shema of Deut. 6:4 and then immediately follows it with the call to love one's neighbor as oneself. In other words, love for God will translate into sensitive care and concern for others. Discipleship is not only about relationship with God but also about how that relationship makes for better relationships with others. The concluding remark is that all the law and prophets depend on this.

A similar answer to the same question is commended by Jesus in the Luke 10:25–28 passage. That text also contains the parable of the good Samaritan, giving an example of what Jesus means. So the point is that one is to care for a neighbor in need, to be ready to serve. Jesus also is underscoring that neighbors can come from surprising places. So he tells the querying scribe to go and do likewise.

Yet another passage emphasizes this ethical base: Matt. 19:16–30// Mark 10:17–31 (like Luke 18:18–30). Here the issue is about the reception of eternal life. The initial reply comes in terms of the commands of the second half of the Ten Commandments, the portion treating human relationships. It is fascinating that this would be the initial response to a question about having eternal life. To emphasize the second half of the Decalogue apparently assumes that the first half is also honored, but in responding this way the link between honoring God and loving others is emphasized. After these remarks about others, the rest of the answer about having eternal life comes in terms of allying oneself to Jesus and his cause, but the two ideas should not be disconnected. To ally oneself to Jesus and follow him means that God will be loved and that as a result one's neighbor will be treated with love and integrity as well. That is part of the practical result of what turning to God in the call of Jesus involves.

Luke sets up this point in the ministry of John the Baptist, where the prophet's work and call to repentance also realigns relationships to God and especially to others (Luke 3:7–14). Every reply for what the crowd is to do if they repent deals with how they conduct their relationships or how they pursue their vocation. Repentance impacts not merely how they walk with God but also how they interact with people.

Luke and Matthew make the point again in texts that call for love of enemies (Matt. 5:43–48; Luke 6:27–36). In Matthew, vengeance and retaliation specifically are ruled out, as Jesus heightens the call of God. Love, mercy, grace, and service are to characterize the disciple who loves because of the experience of being forgiven and being the object of mercy.

Matthew has two additional texts that focus on the question of mercy, something that Luke has already pointed to in the call to imitate the mercy of the Father in Luke 6:35–36. The debate over Jesus's associations with tax collectors and sinners along with a Sabbath incident generate remarks about God desiring mercy, not sacrifice (Matt. 9:9–13; 12:1–8; cf. Hosea 6:6).

The character of Jesus's ministry to those on the fringe, especially highlighted in Luke, also supports this theme. Here Luke 14:7–24 is important. Jesus calls for his audience to invite the poor, maimed, lame, and blind to the banquet, those who cannot give back in kind. This shows the breadth of Jesus's call to reach out, stretching beyond tax collectors and sinners, who are the objects of fellowship in certain texts (Luke 5:27–32). The scope of these relationships means that social class or status do not matter in terms of who is served.

In John, this call is present in two key texts. The exchange over the woman caught in adultery shows how Jesus introduces sinners to forgiveness while calling them to righteousness (John 7:52–8:11). Mercy is first extended to the woman, but the goal of righteousness is not ignored. The tone of Luke 7:36–50, with its commendation of the anointing by the sinful woman, is similar.

The second Johannine text is the "new commandment," putting a premium on the disciples' love for one another as a testimony to being Jesus's followers (John 13:34–35). It is this call and standard that in part leads Jesus to call for disciples to have a righteousness that exceeds that of the Pharisees or to be "perfect" as the Father is perfect. A concern for this standard of love producing a unity in the community also drives Jesus's prayer in John 17, where such a response expresses knowing God and experiencing eternal life (John

17:3, 13–26). Such unity is important as a witness to the world of the difference Jesus makes. As John will later put it in one of his letters, "We love, because he first loved us" (1 John 4:19). Paul expresses the same idea in teaching that we have been designed to walk in love and unity (Eph. 4–5). The other dimension of this is Jesus's call to walk in integrity of heart, as seen in the antitheses of Matt. 5:21–48.

Righteous Integrity

The disciples' character is also a focus of Jesus's teaching. The disciples should live as lights and honor God (Matt. 5:14–16). Jesus's exposition of the law in Matt. 5:21–48 intensifies the Torah into an exhortation for what the citizen of the kingdom should be like from the heart. Here the issues are not just murder but also anger, not just adultery but also lust, not divorce but faithfulness to a commitment, not oath taking but truthfulness, not retaliation but serving vulnerably, not hatred or selective love but unconditional love and prayer. Life is to be lived in a way that is distinct from how Gentiles typically live, in which one gives love only to those from whom love is received. It is this integrity of character that mirrors God (also Luke 6:35–36).

The emphasis on what comes from the heart also appears when Jesus speaks about what truly defiles (Matt. 15:10–20//Mark 7:14–23). So the exposition of the law by Jesus in Matt. 5 as well as in these defilement texts is not about an emphasis on keeping all the law's stipulations but on the character the law intends to help impact. All of the focus in these texts is on the heart and character of the disciple versus issues tied to practices associated with worship at the temple or matters tied to issues of ritual cleanliness. It is what comes out of the heart that defiles, not what one puts in the body. In a parenthetical reflection of the evangelist, Mark 7:19 states that Jesus declared all foods clean by what he says as recorded in Mark 7:1–23. Matthew 15:20 says hands cannot defile because it is not what one puts into the body that defiles but what comes out of the heart. The list of vices reveals a defiled heart. It parallels what Paul describes in Gal. 5:19–21, with the fruit of the Spirit providing the contrastive virtues in 5:22–23. With these virtues in place, there is no need for law.

The negative counterexample of this call to integrity is seen in Jesus's rebuke of the scribes and Pharisees in the woes he pronounces against them in two different texts: Matt. 23 and Luke 11:37–52. Here the negative example to avoid is hypocrisy, pride, and a kind of self-deceiving pseudospirituality, where mercy and justice and faithfulness are ignored and the corrupt inner person is concealed by what the external person portrays.

Jesus's emphasis on the fruit of the disciple also fits in here. Fruit is the goal of his ministry when seed is sown or a vineyard is planted (Matt. 13:23//Mark 4:20//Luke 8:15; Matt. 12:33–37//Luke 6:43–45).

So Jesus makes the call to righteousness from the heart in many ways. The array of themes pointing to the same goal are multiply attested across the tradition about Jesus's teaching.

Possessions and the World

Jesus has much to say against devotion to the world and to possessions. His warning, encased within the parable of the sower, is about the threat to fruitfulness (Matt. 13:22//Mark 4:19//Luke 8:14). The seed of God's word about the kingdom can be cut off from being fruitful because of the devil, the worries of the world, or persecution. Only a heart that embraces the word with patience and perseverance yields fruit (Luke 8:15). Jesus's call to trust God makes the point that resting in God's care means that one does not need to be anxious about such concerns as food or clothing (Matt. 6:25–34//Luke 12:22–32).

Several other texts make the point strongly that possessions can be an obstacle to God and can create a hard heart toward others. So in the exchange with the rich man, Jesus points out how difficult it is for a rich man to enter the kingdom (Matt. 19:23//Mark 10:23//Luke 18:24).

Numerous parables in Luke likewise underscore this concern and warning. Jesus's concern about material things and their use appears in the parable of the rich fool (Luke 12:13–21) and in the parable about stewardship with its following remarks (Luke 16:1–13).

In Luke 12 all the rich man can think of is himself and what the resources he has been blessed with can do for him. The parable's multiple use of the first-person pronoun shows this force. This parable also explains how riches and greed can become idolatry as we become the center of the world, focused on what things and people can do for us.

Luke 16 is not just about money but also about any form of possession, as the term "mammon" indicates. Ethically, the point about hard-heartedness and its spiritual risks surface in the scene involving the rich man and Lazarus (Luke 16:19–31). After Lazarus goes to blessing and the rich man is confined to Hades, the rich man only thinks Lazarus is there to serve him. "Send Lazarus" to relieve "my" pain, he asks. People are objects of service to him. In his lifetime, when the circumstances were reversed, the rich man did nothing to help Lazarus or serve him, so now it is too late. The text declares that this ethic is what the law and the prophets teach. No one should need a voice from beyond, which ironically the parable supplies while denying it in the story (16:30–31), to remind them of this ethical responsibility.

In contrast stands Jesus's praise of the widow who in offering her meager copper coins, a mere couple of pennies, gives of her very life to God (Mark 12:41–44//Luke 21:1–4). By offering in a way that clearly shows sacrifice, she reflects her priorities and commitment to honor God.

Another positive example is the repentant rich man Zacchaeus. He serves as a model for handling wealth because he now is generous with his possessions and fully rights the wrongs that he previously committed (Luke 19:1–10). He repays to the full penalty of the law and does so without coercion.

In one sense, the problem with attachment to possessions is that it reflects independence from God and excessive union with the world, which is an affront to God. To gain the world but lose the soul is a tragedy (Matt. 16:26//Mark 8:36//Luke 9:25, like John 12:25).

John's Gospel makes this point by declaring that the world's hatred of Jesus will carry over to his disciples and that his disciples are not of this world (John 7:7; 8:23; 15:18–19; 16:20, 33; 17:14). The world does not understand Jesus or what he represents (John 14:17). Jesus has taken his disciples out of the world's approach to living, but they are still to engage the world, protected by God, since the separation involves only a different set of values and way to live

(John 17:15–19). They are his special objects of prayer as he calls them to face rejection in the world rather than isolate themselves from it (John 17:6, 9). This leads into the next subtheme: suffering.

Suffering

In the world, bearing the cross is the mark of the disciple. Jesus did not teach a triumphalism of victory in the current era. Vindication and triumph await his return. Now the disciples' call is to share in the rejection that Jesus met. The community functioning as a minority is when it is most effective.

The texts just mentioned from John's Gospel make this point. However, the clearest text on suffering appears just after Peter confesses Jesus to be the Christ at Caesarea Philippi. Here Jesus immediately turns to preach about his impending suffering and to call the disciples to be prepared to share the same road of shame and rejection (Matt. 16:24–27//Mark 8:34–38//Luke 9:23–26). In Luke Jesus urges the crowds to "count the cost" of this discipleship, which will not be easy (Luke 14:25–33). In other texts Jesus speaks of how the decision for him may split families (Matt. 10:34–39//Luke 12:51–53). He offers encouragement by revealing that fearing God and acknowledging the Son of Man will lead to the disciple's being acknowledged before God (Matt. 10:26–33//Luke 12:1–12). In the Olivet Discourse Jesus promises that the persecution to come and the Spirit's enablement will allow disciples to testify on the gospel's behalf (Matt. 24:9–14// Mark 13:9–13//Luke 21:12–19). Those who trust in God will endure (Luke 21:19).

Service-Mission

This ethical call to suffering and the risk that it includes do not mean that disciples are to withdraw from the world as the Jewish community at Qumran did. Jesus has sent disciples out into the world to serve it as an example, being like salt and light that draw attention to God's goodness (Matt. 5:13–16; John 17:11, 15). Whether it is seen in the mission of the disciples during Jesus's ministry (Matt. 10; Luke 9:1–6; 10:1–23) or in the commissions that conclude Matthew and Luke and begin Acts (Matt. 28:18–20; Luke 24:44–49; Acts 1:8), the call of the disciple is to take the message of God's deliverance and forgiveness, along with the message of how one should live before God, into all the nations (Mark 13:10; 14:9). It is parallel to Jesus's call to enter into rest and give life's heavy burden to him (Matt. 11:28–30). In addition, the example of Jesus's general compassion to outsiders, as shown in his healing ministry, also indicates that acts of compassion testify to the caring character of God.

Summary

Jesus defines his mission as that of the Servant who calls out to the captives to experience release (Luke 4:16–19). Everything about the character of Jesus's ministry wedded together words and deeds of compassion and showed the love of God standing behind his preaching of divine forgiveness and mercy. What Jesus proclaimed, he also concretely displayed through his ministry. This was no mere social gospel; it was a showing forth of the fully rounded gospel of God's kingdom, evidencing concretely God's care for people.

The presence of the offer of forgiveness and mercy does not mean that salvation is automatic for everyone. Jesus formed a new community of those who wished to walk in what soon became known as "the Way" (Acts 9:2; 18:25; 19:9). It was to be made up of Jews and eventually Gentiles who came to Jesus in a faith that had turned them to God out of a sense of spiritual need for deliverance and forgiveness. This showed their desire to live life by reflecting God's image in them as humankind was originally designed to function. By embracing God and his love, they took on a commitment to love God and their neighbor, taking the message of this fresh walk into eternal life and, by word and deed, delivering it to a needy but rejecting world. They joined together in community, accepting all the risk of suffering that this entailed. But not everyone would respond. The suffering would be great, with some even losing their lives. Yet questions remained: Where was justice in living with that tension? When would God resolve the need for justice to be dispensed? These questions raise the final major theme of salvation, justice, and the vindication to come.

7

The Vindication to Come: Warning to Israel, Gentile Inclusion, and the Son of Man's Return to Judge

Accountability, Justice, and Deliverance to Come

Judgment texts can be divided into two types: (1) those that speak of judgment in general, and (2) those that describe the activity of the Son of Man.

This theme is a major component of Jesus's teaching, as a textual listing shows.[1]

Mark: 3:28–29 (//Matt. 12:31–32//Luke 12:10); 4:24 (//Matt. 7:2// Luke 6:38); 4:25, 29; 6:11 (//Matt. 10:14//Luke 9:5); 8:38 (//Matt.

1. For a comprehensive study of this theme minus Son of Man texts, see Marius Reiser, *Jesus and Judgment: The Eschatological Proclamation in Its Jewish Context*, trans. Linda M. Maloney (Minneapolis: Fortress, 1997). A text is described as "like" another if the passage is not clearly a true parallel yet may have a similar theme or is in a clearly distinct context.

10:32–33//Luke 12:8–9); 9:43–49 (like Matt. 5:29–30); 10:25 (//Matt. 19:24//Luke 18:25); 10:31 (//Matt. 19:30); 12:1–12 (//Matt. 21:33–46//Luke 20:9–19, 40); 13:4, 13, 20, 24–27 (with parallels in Matt. 24 and Luke 21); 14:62 (//Matt. 26:64; like Luke 22:69).

Teaching material common to Matthew and Luke (i.e., Q): Matt. 7:1–2//Luke 6:37–38; Matt. 7:13–14 (like Luke 13:23–24); Matt. 7:22–23 (like Luke 13:25–27); Matt. 7:24–27//Luke 6:47–49; Matt. 8:11–12 (like Luke 13:28–29); Matt. 10:14//Luke 9:5; Matt. 10:15 (like Luke 10:12); Matt. 10:28 (like Luke 12:4–5); Matt. 10:32 (like Luke 12:8–9); Matt. 10:39 (like Luke 17:33); Matt. 11:6//Luke 7:23; Matt. 11:21–24 (like Luke 10:13–15); Matt. 12:27//Luke 11:19; Matt. 12:32//Luke 12:10; Matt. 12:41–42//Luke 11:31–32; Matt. 19:28 (like Luke 22:28–30); Matt. 23:34–36 (like Luke 11:49–51); Matt. 23:37–39 (like Luke 13:34–35); Matt. 24:37–39 (like Luke 17:26–29); Matt. 24:40–41 (like Luke 17:34–35); Matt. 24:45–51 (like Luke 12:42–46); Matt. 25:11–12 (like Luke 13:25); Matt. 25:14–30 (like Luke 19:11–27); Luke 11:30 (like Matt. 12:40); Luke 14:16–24 (like Matt. 22:2–14).

Matthew only: 5:4, 7, 22; 7:19, 21; 8:29; 12:36–37; 13:24–30, 36–43, 47–50; 15:13; 18:14, 23–35; 21:43; 23:33; 25:31–46.

Luke only: 6:21, 24–26; 10:20; 12:48–49, 58–59; 13:2–5, 6–9; 14:11; 16:1–8, 19–31.[2]

Clearly, the theme of judgment is widely distributed in the Gospel material. While Jesus's general remarks about judgment often serve to warn national Israel of its risk, the Son of Man sayings move in a more comprehensive direction. I treat these themes in this sequence.

2. Ibid., 303, says that this comprises 37 verses in Mark (or 22 percent of Jesus's discourse material in this Gospel), 76 verses of Q (or 35 percent of Q material), 60 verses of Matthean special material (64 percent of Matthew's discourse material), and 37 verses in Luke's unique material (28 percent of Luke's special material). My list does not match Reiser's numbers exactly because I note parallel texts more fully, but the figures are generally similar. They reveal how important this theme is for Jesus, in contrast to the Jesus Seminar's claim that Jesus did not teach about judgment. This is yet another indication of how apocalyptic Jesus's teaching was.

Warning to Israel and Gentile Inclusion

Many of Jesus's general remarks about judgment are designed to challenge Israel to respond to the promise he offers by reversing expectations they had about who would receive blessing. Thus Matt. 12:41–42//Luke 11:31–32 reports Jesus's remark that the queen of the South and the people of Nineveh will rise up at the judgment as witnesses against this generation and condemn it for failing to see that one greater than Solomon or Jonah is present. Two features are important in this warning. First is that Gentiles are portrayed as being more responsive than Jews (a similar theme appears in Luke 4:24–27). Second is that the issue of a lack of responsiveness focuses on the person of Jesus, not just on what he teaches. His person should be embraced because he is greater than the king of wisdom (Solomon) and is more important than a prophet like Jonah.[3] Those who insist that Jesus merely taught about the kingdom and did not feature himself mistakenly dismiss texts like these and ignore the significance of Jesus's actions.

Similar in tone is a second text. In Matt. 11:21–24//Luke 10:13–15 Jesus declares that the judgment will be more tolerable for the wicked Gentile cities of Tyre and Sidon than for Chorazin and Bethsaida, while Capernaum will be brought down to Sheol. In favor of the authenticity of this saying is that Chorazin is an obscure town that appears nowhere else in the Gospel tradition. If the saying were a later creation of the church put onto Jesus's lips, why would it highlight a town of no significance? In Matthew, Jesus goes on to state that even a place like Sodom would have responded to such an opportunity to repent. Hard-heartedness about Jesus's call to repent will meet with judgment. So both well-known and obscure towns are included in Jesus's warning about the consequences of rejecting his message.

A third warning to Israel that includes the provocative note of Gentile inclusion appears in Matt. 8:11–12//Luke 13:28–29. Here the image is of people coming from east and west (Luke adds north and south) to sit at the banquet table of the kingdom while the "children

3. Ibid., 219–20, defends the authenticity of this saying, including its open but indirect Christology, which he argues would not be the approach of a text created by the church.

of the kingdom" (Matt. 8:12 KJV) or "you yourselves" (Luke) are thrust out into "outer darkness" (Matthew), where there is weeping and gnashing of teeth.[4] Again the warning is to Israel for its refusal to recognize Jesus as the Christ, with the disturbing note that Gentiles, even many of the Gentiles, will fare better.

A fourth text with the same themes is the parable of the rejected invitation to the feast in Matt. 22:2–14//Luke 14:16–24. Some interpreters hold that the image of the new invitees does not suggest an outreach to Gentiles. However, the pattern of these texts as a group argues in favor of an allusion to them. Here it is the fringe *plus* the Gentiles who are seen as "in," while those originally invited miss the banquet, which comes now and is not postponed until later. Rejecting the invitation now and not responding results in missing the blessing of the kingdom.

Repentance is important for escaping judgment, as explained in Luke 13:1–9. Here the issue is whether a judgment through a social tragedy or a natural disaster is indicative of the presence of judgment on "worse" sinners. Jesus does not answer that question; instead he warns that without repentance all will perish. This warning to individuals then is made more corporate by a parable in which a fig tree, picturing Israel, fails to yield fruit. The parable argues that the nation has only a short time left to respond. The image of the separating judgment in John the Baptist's teaching and in Jesus's kingdom parables makes a similar point (Matt. 3:7–12//Luke 3:7–9, 16–17; Mark 4:29, like Matt. 9:37//Luke 10:2; Matt. 10:14).

Finally, that Israel is a focus of this judgment also is seen in Matt. 19:28 (like Luke 22:28–30), where Jesus's chosen disciples sit as judges over Israel. These texts underscore the fact that Jesus had a special ministry to Israel and held that nation especially accountable for how it reacted to him, even at times trying to shame his people with the prospect that the hated Gentiles would fare better in the judgment to come. In these texts the issue is a proper response to Jesus and his message, which requires turning to God and embracing the kingdom that Jesus brings in a way that leads to bearing fruit. So people had

4. Both expressions, "outer darkness" and "weeping and gnashing of teeth," are figures associated with being rejected in judgment (ibid., 236–39). On darkness, see *1 En.* 10.4; 10.8; *Jub.* 7.29; *Pss. Sol.* 14.9; 15.10.

better get their accounts sorted out with God (Luke 12:57–59) and also, as beneficiaries of grace and forgiveness, be ready to show the same mercy to others (Matt. 18:23–35).

Also significant is the prediction of judgment in the short term for Israel, which also pictures the chaos of events leading to the return. In the Olivet Discourse Jesus predicts the destruction of the temple (Mark 13//Matt. 24//Luke 21:5–37). The prediction is rooted in covenantal unfaithfulness, which leads to judgment by the nations, as Deut. 28–32 had warned. The discourse not only predicts temple destruction in the short term but also uses this picture of international chaos to mirror what events at the end will look like. The text is a pattern prophecy, where events in the short term mirror ultimate fulfillment as well. Many of the key Son of Man judgment images emerge from this discourse.

This warning of judgment upon Israel raises the question of the future of this people in the program of God. It is often suggested that the presence of promise in Christ and the church leaves Israel on the outside looking in. Passages like Matt. 8:11–12//Luke 13:28–29 certainly leave that impression; so does the picture of the temple's destruction as an eschatological pattern. Yet things are not so simple. Those texts may well be aimed at specific generations of Israel rather than depicting the situation at the end.

Many reasons exist for thinking that Israel might have a future in God's program. First is the issue of God's faithfulness. This is not a point that Jesus's teaching raises but one that comes from Paul's discussion of Israel in Rom. 9–11. Here Paul is expressly speaking of Israel as those for whom he weeps, and he wishes himself accursed so they might be saved. This is not a reference to the church but to natural branches currently cut out and excluded from the blessing. In Rom. 11 he anticipates their being grafted back in at some future point. The prospect leads him to praise the promises of God, which are irrevocable. From where did Paul acquire this sense of ongoing hope?

Jesus's teaching seems to provide the source. In Luke 13:34–35//Matt. 23:37–39 Jesus declares Israel to be under exilic-like judgment *until* Israel says, "Blessed is he who comes in the name of the Lord!" The declaration that Israel's house is desolate recalls language from

Jer. 22:5 and 12:7. Judgment like that of the exile is not permanent. This appeal to recognizing the one whom God has sent comes from Ps. 118, which Jesus uses to discuss the suffering and exaltation of the promised one. He anticipates that the nation will reject him, but only for a time. Language in Luke 21:20–24 speaks of Jerusalem being trampled down "*until* the times of the Gentiles are fulfilled" (emphasis added). The contrast to the times of the Gentiles would be a time for Israel. One day Jerusalem will be redeemed as God fulfills his commitments to the nation.

The early church's expectation of a restoration for Israel, even after Jesus was raised and had expounded the hope of the Hebrew Scriptures to them, reinforces the idea that this is the proper reading of the theme (Acts 1:6–7; 3:18–22).

So a warning of judgment to Israel holds each generation accountable for their rejection of Jesus but does not preclude that one day they will respond favorably to him. Even more, Gentile inclusion does not mean Israelite exclusion. God can expand the promise without excluding the original recipients. The scene of Gentiles streaming into kingdom fellowship, with many in Israel on the outside, is a picture that is true of many generations, but it is not permanent. The destruction of the temple in the short term does not mean that people will not be able to stream to Jerusalem to worship one day, as texts like Isa. 2:2–4 argue. The hopes of the nations and of Israel are shared in the reconciliation that Jesus's work brings at the national level; thus Isa. 19:16–25 portrays Egypt, Assyria, and Israel all sharing in the worship of God together. Nothing in Jesus's teaching should make us think that original hope revealed by God has been altered. The apostolic testimony goes in this direction by affirming restoration for the nation as well as for the world (Acts 3:18–22, as the Hebrew Scriptures promise; 26:6–7, "the promise . . . our twelve tribes hope to obtain"; 28:20, "the hope of Israel"; Rom. 9–11; Eph. 2:11–22). What grows out of the resurrection, which Paul defends in Acts, is a restorative theology that brings Israel and the nations together in peace. The direction for this hope was set in the Hebrew Scriptures, as Acts 3:18–22 affirms, and by Jesus's own teaching. Israel is judged until its people respond (Luke 13:34–35//Matt. 23:37–39), a point that holds out hope for ethnic Israel's response as a mass of people.

The Judgment of the Son of Man

More comprehensive in scope are the Son of Man judgment texts and the judgment imagery emerging from the kingdom parables, especially several unique parables in Matt. 13.

These kingdom parables make clear that although Israel is a focus (Mark 12:1–12//Matt. 21:33–46//Luke 20:9–19), the ultimate scope of Jesus's rule extends across the entire earth (Matt. 13:24–30, 36–43).[5] The fact that Jesus's rule will extend across all the earth helps to explain why the role of the land of Israel is less prominent in the NT. When there is peace and Christ's rule extends over all the earth, protecting borders becomes less of an issue.[6]

In the crucially important parable of the wheat and darnel (or "weeds"; Matt. 13:24–30, 36–43), Jesus clarifies that kingdom authority extends to "the field" of the "world." Thus kingdom authority and judgment are comprehensive and come at the "close of the age." The executor of the judgment is the Son of Man, who carries it out in the presence of the angels. The result is a dividing of humanity into the righteous, who shine as light in the kingdom, and the evildoers, who are cast into fire, where there is weeping and gnashing of teeth. The point is made again in less elaborate detail in the parable of the net (Matt. 13:47–50). The kingdom has a claim on every soul whom God has created. Accountability comes one day. The idea that we are completely independent beings is excluded by this theme. Each person will face God one day.

The judgment rotates around two themes: (1) the performance of righteousness, tightly linked to (2) a person's recognition of the Son of Man. Whereas the kingdom parables speak of (1) doing righteousness, the Son of Man sayings tend to highlight (2) embracing the

5. Reiser, *Jesus and Judgment*, 238–39, points out how Jesus's imagery of judgment deals not with a transcendent kingdom hope but one expressed on this earth and in history. This point is well made. Yet Reiser's failure to treat Son of Man texts leads to inadequate appreciation for the comprehensiveness of Jesus's claim to judge the world, as well as understating the nature of hope for Gentile inclusion anticipated in these texts.

6. By analogy, compare how the French and German border functioned in World War II with how it functions now, as the two nations are a part of the European Union.

Son of Man, although the theme of judgment tied to righteousness also appears (Matt. 16:27//Mark 8:38//Luke 9:26).

Matthew alone highlights the judgment's attachment to the standard of "according to one's deed" (AT; singular in Greek). A decision about the Son of Man seems to be in view here as "the deed." Mark and Luke speak of "being ashamed of [Jesus]." The point may well be that response to Jesus leads to righteousness.[7]

A key text here is Matt. 10:32–33//Luke 12:8–9. Whoever acknowledges the Son before humanity (i.e., to embrace and testify to him) receives the promise that the Son of Man will acknowledge the respondent before the angels in judgment. The linkage between the idea of righteousness and responding to Jesus is seen most vividly in the parable of the judgment of the nations (Matt. 25:31–46). Here it is the treatment of those tied to Jesus with acts of service and compassion that allows one to be a "sheep" and enter into the kingdom. In the parable the assumption is that embracing Jesus leads to a change of heart and of behavior that God will honor. This is not unlike the emphasis that one sees in John the Baptist as one who prepared the way. There repentance was expressed not just in terms of how one walks with God but also by how others are treated or in connection with images that picture reconciliation between people (Luke 1:16–17; 3:10–14). This same emphasis is also assumed in the Sermons on the Mount and on the Plain (Matt. 5–7; Luke 6:20–49).[8]

The apocalyptic Son of Man sayings tend to surface toward the end of Jesus's ministry. As Jesus neared Jerusalem and prepared to meet his fate there, he began to discuss what would follow his death and vindication. Jesus's resurrection was about vindication, but so also will be his return.

The eschatological discourse material is key here (Matt. 24–25; Mark 13; Luke 17:22–37; 21:5–38).[9] The judgment will come suddenly.

7. In Paul, Rom. 6 and 8 make this linkage emphatically.

8. The same point was made in the subsection "Kingdom and Ethics" in chap. 3 above.

9. The theme here is the final judgment. As already noted, this discourse is a "pattern" prophecy in which the judgment on Israel and the destruction of the temple (predicted for AD 70) are seen as a microcosm of the way final judgment proceeds. After all, Jesus's observation about the temple's destruction triggers the discourse. That AD 70 is not the only event referred to here is seen in the remarks about

Other texts speak of it as a thief in the night (Luke 12:39//Matt. 24:43), coming at an unexpected hour (Luke 12:40//Matt. 24:44), appearing instantly and like lightning (Luke 17:24//Matt. 24:27), or coming as in the days of Noah and Lot and suddenly interrupting everyday life (Luke 17:26–30//Matt. 24:37–41).

Beyond general signs of religious, political, and natural chaos, Jesus gives no calendrical detail. Rather, these texts stress the point that the judgment's uncertain timing and the accountability it brings require that one be alert, faithful, and always prepared (Luke 12:35–48, like Matt. 24:43–51; Matt. 25:1–13). It may well take longer to come than they might hope (Luke 17:22; 18:8). The tension between the coming occurring next and even soon yet after so long that people will yearn for it is never resolved in Jesus's teaching. He simply affirms both realities while highlighting that the timing of the return is known by the Father alone (Mark 13:32). This coming leads the nations to mourn, for it is a judgment that extends over the entire earth, with the unrighteous and unresponsive headed for condemnation (Matt. 24:30//Mark 13:26//Luke 21:27). The vindication involves the Son of Man coming with divine judgment authority, as indicated by his association with riding the clouds, an image from Dan. 7, an act that only God performs (Ps. 68:4).

Another key text is Jesus's reply at the Jewish examination of him (Mark 14:62//Matt. 26:64, like Luke 22:69). Key to this description of vindication is the declaration of Jesus's total divine authority to judge even the Jewish leadership. Jesus makes this claim as one who is to be seen at God's right hand and coming on the clouds with final judgment authority. This theme also appears in John, but with less

---

unprecedented tribulation in the Matthean and Markan versions of the discourse, which show that their Gospels are highlighting the end judgment, in contrast to Luke, who highlights the nearer events tied to the type. Failure to read this discourse as a pattern prophecy dealing with two time periods that mirror each other leads to all kinds of confusion about what is taught here. This confusion usually shows itself as forcing one to choose whether AD 70 or the end is in view, or by conflating both as having taken place with the destruction of the temple in AD 70. Also, the theme of gathering together those who believe precludes an exclusive reference to AD 70. See the detailed discussion of these passages in Darrell L. Bock, *Jesus according to Scripture: Restoring the Portrait from the Gospels* (Grand Rapids: Baker Academic, 2002), §§245–53.

emphasis. John 5:27 has Jesus speak of being given "authority to judge because he is the Son of Man" (NIV). Here as well the judgment to come is based both on one's righteousness and on one's response to Jesus (John 5:24, 28–29). Jesus also speaks of his words being a judge on the last day, underscoring the authority of his teaching (John 12:48). A narrative remark in John likewise focuses the judgment on how one responds to Jesus's message (John 3:18–19).

Summary

The picture of the Son of Man as judge does not detail the timing, other than that judgment comes in association with return and the end of the age.[10] More important for Jesus is the idea that judgment and eschatological hope show that everyone is accountable to God and must be ready to settle accounts with him.

No theme shows the centrality of Jesus's person and authority more than his being responsible for the final judgment. Here Jesus's favorite title, Son of Man, comes into play, drawing on the imagery of Dan. 7 to make the point that the one whom God promised would have such authority. In fact, the Son of Man has come both in ministry and to suffer, as his earthly ministry shows. The journey to the cross and what resulted from the resurrection point to Jesus assuming such a role in God's plan. The fact that Jesus was taken from the earth up will allow him to come down from heaven one day and weigh human accounts. To conclude this study, we now turn to the events and teaching of the crucial last week, which led to Jesus's death and resurrection.

10. In considering the doctrine of the "end times," issues of timing and detail are addressed through consideration of other texts, in both the OT and the NT, that present the contents of this consummative era. Thus Peter speaks of the return of Jesus leading to the completion of all that the OT already had taught (Acts 3:18–22). The christological point in judgment is that God has appointed one (Jesus) to be the judge of the living and the dead. This is a message that Luke shows to be the way the gospel was summarized to Gentile audiences that did not know the OT (Acts 10:42–43; 17:31) and so could not appreciate who the Son of Man is. Of course, for the NT the "end times" started with the coming of Jesus to earth (Luke 16:16).

8

Jesus's Final Week: A Dispute over Authority

How God Acted from the Earth Up to Vindicate Jesus

This survey of Jesus's theology and ministry closes by focusing attention briefly on the events of the crucial last week of his ministry as the Gospels present them. Those events involve confrontation and debate about who Jesus is. In the sequence God speaks last in resurrection and vindication to show which side of the debate reflects the divine perspective.

This sequence of key events led into Jesus's arrest, trials, conviction, and crucifixion. Most of the early events of the final week produced controversy. The unity of the narrative at this point magnifies the importance of these events. The tightness of sequence between these events associated with this last week allows the thrust of the disputes surrounding Jesus to come into greater focus. One of the mistakes often made in looking at the events tied to Jesus is that the sequencing of events is pulled apart, with each scene assessed one piece at a time. This kind of divide-and-conquer skepticism separates events whose sequence and interrelationship matter.[1] We may miss how the shadow of one event impacts a following event. So a concise look at how these events tie together is important.

By the time of the last week, the Jewish leaders had made their own assessment of Jesus's claims and had rejected them. They had been exposed to Jesus's teaching, which our study has covered, and had rejected Jesus's claims to unique authority. Thus Jesus irritated the religious leaders in both major and minor ways. His Sabbath acts, his association with sinners, his teaching on purity, his claims to forgive sin, and his perceived lack of piety had all brought suspicion against Jesus even before his climactic entry into Jerusalem on the back of a donkey with disciples lauding him as Israel's hope.[2] The last week does not happen in a vacuum. What already has taken place set up the strong reaction of the leadership during this crucial week.

In turn, Jesus reacted to the leadership's assessment with pronouncements about the nation. He had warned and continued to warn them of the consequences of their failure to embrace God's initiative toward them through him (Luke 13:34–35//Matt. 23:37–39, like Luke 19:41–44). The city and nation were at risk of judgment like Israel experienced when they were led into exile. Spiritual dullness would perpetuate the exile that also had led John the Baptist and Jesus to originally call the nation to repentance so that deliverance could come.

At the center of the dispute stood Jesus's claims of authority as the unique representative of God in bringing kingdom hope. The hope

1. Two studies work through many of these events in detail and defend their historical authenticity. See Darrell L. Bock and Robert L. Webb, eds., *Key Events in the Life of the Historical Jesus: A Collaborative Exploration of Context and Coherence* (Tübingen: Mohr Siebeck, 2009), 383–853, representing half of the twelve events covered in the entire volume that come from this final week—including the entry into Jerusalem, the temple incident, the Last Supper, the Jewish examination of Jesus, the trial by Pilate leading to crucifixion, and the resurrection. The same ground is covered more concisely in Darrell L. Bock, *Who Is Jesus? Linking the Historical Jesus with the Christ of Faith* (New York: Howard Books, 2012), 107–214. Here now we simply give an overview of the sequence of these last-week core events, summarize their significance, and add notes about controversies that the last week generated.

2. To show these elements and how they worked to raise tensions, see Darrell L. Bock, "What Did Jesus Do That Got Him into Trouble? Jesus in the Continuum of Early Judaism–Early Christianity," in *Jesus in Continuum*, ed. Tom Holmén, WUNT 289 (Tübingen: Mohr Siebeck, 2012), 171–210.

was only active for those who recognized who Jesus was and accepted that his mission of deliverance was real and from God. As the week concluded, on top of all this ultimately stood the empty tomb and the events tied to it. It is here that Jesus ceased to be a failed dead prophet and was revealed to be far more to his disciples. To understand the importance of the resurrection and the claims associated with it, one must appreciate the debate surrounding the final week of Jesus's life. This overview of the key elements of the week starts with Jesus's entrance into Jerusalem.

Entry into Jerusalem

Jesus entered the city on a donkey, evoking a claim of kingship through the disciples' praising God's work and the hope of kingship (Matt. 21:1–9//Mark 11:1–10//Luke 19:28–40//John 12:12–16). Although John's Gospel is clear that the significance of this event in terms of Zech. 9:9 is something that the disciples came to appreciate only later, the entry represented a declaration of the arrival of the promised figure in a time of longed-for hope. The entry was the offer of a delivering king to the nation, presented with an air of humility that paralleled the larger suffering and service character of Jesus's ministry.[3] Thus Jesus entered the city not merely as a pilgrim or even as a prophet but as a messianic claimant. All the Gospels underscore the eschatological notes of the entry. In different ways Luke and John report how the Pharisees reacted to this event. In Luke they urge Jesus to stop this proclamation of praise, but Jesus refuses (Luke 19:39–40). In John the emphasis is how popular Jesus is. In John's account the Pharisees sense the threat of his claims.

As Luke alone records, Jesus enters the city quite aware that the leadership will not accept him, a choice eventually precluding the mass of the populace from embracing him. Weeping at the tragedy of it all, he declares that the nation, epitomized by the city, will be

3. For treatment of the OT and Second Temple Jewish background to messianic hope and NT teaching on the same, see Herbert W. Bateman IV, Darrell L. Bock, and Gordon Johnston, *Jesus the Messiah: Tracing the Promises, Expectations, and Coming of Israel's King* (Grand Rapids: Kregel, 2012).

judged because "you did not know the time of your visitation" (Luke 19:41–44).

The aside about the disciples not recognizing the full significance of this event at the time is important (John 12:16). It points to the fact that historical events have depth. Sometimes the import of a happening can be more fully grasped only through subsequent events and reflection. Events have "depth," and sometimes history reveals them in stages as links in a chain, making the import of earlier events clearer. The Gospels are written from this wider perspective. This feature complicates some debates about historicity. Sometimes a single-dimensional read of history leaves the suggestion that what is realized or articulated later is not a genuine historical reflection about an earlier event. By doing so, one may be denying what is implicit in an event that later happenings expose and make more explicit. The entry is one such event that John acknowledges had more to it than the disciples realized at the time. Some of that realization emerged because of what came after the entry. What was appreciated later as part of the historical plotline emerged because of the depth and impact of the last week's starting point. The messianic claims of hope in the entry hung over the city like a shadow during all the events that followed.

The Temple Incident

The next event underscores Jesus's sense of call and identity as he moves into the temple to act against it symbolically by challenging the money changers (Matt. 21:12–13//Mark 11:15–17//Luke 19:45–46). The act was significant because the temple was the central place of worship for Judaism, the most sacred space of the nation, the place where God was said to dwell. It also was believed that in the last days a cleansing of the nation would accompany the messianic times. As one of several texts, *Pss. Sol.* 17–18 looks forward to such hope (esp. 17.21–30 [17.23–27 in some versifications]). The idea of a temple in need of purging or even being rebuilt was a part of Jewish hope (4Q174; 11QT[a] 29.8–10; *1 En.* 90.28–29; Tob. 13:16–17; *Jub.* 1.15–17; *Sib. Or.* 3.286–94; *2 Bar.* 68.5–6; benediction 14 of the Shemoneh Esreh).

This expectation about a temple cleaned or rebuilt is part of the reason why debate exists about whether the act is to be seen as a cleansing or a prediction of destruction. Both can fit the background. However, what often is overlooked is that a prediction of destruction might not have been seen as a permanent act, given the Jewish hope expressed in some texts of a purged temple that also is rebuilt. In a sense, for the nation the end of spiritual exile would come with the arrival of the cleansing of the holy city. In effect, this is what Jesus was claiming to do and, more importantly, to be qualified to do. So the act was an inherent claim for authority to reform Judaism, even down to its most sacred spaces. The act forced a choice. It was a symbolic event that the leadership could not ignore, a direct critique of the way the temple was being operated. This act demanded a response of either embracing the reform Jesus called for or forming a resistance to what it represented.

Final Controversies

The first in a series of controversies underscores the reaction to Jesus's claims of authority. The Jewish leadership asks Jesus where he received the authority to do such things as cleanse the temple (Matt. 21:23–27//Mark 11:27–33//Luke 20:1–8). The question, expressed in the plural ("these things"), means that the objection extends beyond the temple act, yet this appears to have served as the trigger for confronting Jesus.

Jesus replies with a question of his own about the authority of John the Baptist. His question in effect asks whether God can work through someone from outside the nation's socially constituted leadership. The expected reply is that God can and did do this in the case of John. So Jesus's authority is, like John's, rooted in God. Everything about the last week centers around whether or not Jesus is sent from God and the differing opinions on that question.

To drive home the point, Jesus tells a parable about wicked tenants, picturing the Jewish leadership as unfaithful in their response over a long period of Israel's history (Matt. 21:33–46//Mark 12:1–12//Luke 20:9–19). Just as Israel's leaders rejected the prophets sent before Jesus (represented in the parable as the servants), so now they are about to reject God's "beloved son." Here Jesus makes a public claim of his unique relationship to God. The title echoes what heaven said about Jesus at Jesus's baptism and at the transfiguration. No one before or since has occupied this unique position, and yet those given stewardship over the people of God will move to kill God's beloved son. This will result in judgment, with the care of the vineyard passing on to others. In other words, Jesus is the rejected cornerstone that will be exalted by God, regardless of opposition by these leaders. Once again the point is a dispute about authority, with a note that suffering is also a part of the plan for the chosen one.

Other disputes follow about taxes and resurrection. However, the final dispute is a question to ponder (Matt. 22:41–46//Mark 12:35–37//Luke 20:41–44): Why does the patriarch David call his son "Lord" in a society in which respect goes to the ancestor, not to a son? Using Ps. 110:1, Jesus makes the point that the Messiah is not merely David's son but is really his Lord. The title again raises the note of authority. The question lingers about what type of Lord is in view. The scene before the Jewish leaders and the resurrection will supply the answer to that core christological question.

Olivet Discourse

Jesus's authority is also the key point in the eschatological discourse predicting both the destruction of the temple (AD 70) and the later return of the Son of Man to redeem his own and judge the world (Matt. 24–25//Mark 13//Luke 21:5–37). This teaching, although given privately, points to the comprehensive scope of Jesus's relationship to God. He is the one who gives the final judgment. All are accountable to him.

The Last Supper

Jesus's authority shows itself again privately when at the Last Supper he alters a sacred meal originally about Passover and gives it an interpretation tied to his upcoming rejection and death (Matt. 26:26–29//Mark 14:22–25//Luke 21:14–23). Here a celebration of the original salvation of the nation is turned into a ceremony commemorating the inauguration of a new covenant and ultimate salvation. Jesus compares his upcoming work to a sacrifice that makes the new era possible by providing an efficacious offering for those who acknowledge him. The uniqueness of his calling and person is underscored here.

The Jewish Examination of Jesus

Jesus's authoritative claims and acts, many of which were made in public, led the leadership to arrest Jesus. For both political and religious reasons, the leadership wanted Jesus stopped.

According to the Gospel accounts, the key issue at his trial ended up focusing on these claims of authority. After failing to secure charges tied to Jesus's remarks about destroying the temple, as Matthew and Mark make clear, the issue became Jesus's messianic role (Matt. 26:57–62//Mark 14:53–60). The goal here was to formulate a charge that could be translated into political terms against which Rome would need to react. The Romans would not care about a religious dispute as long as Roman rule was not threatened, but they did care about people claiming to be a king. That was Rome's role, they thought. If a prediction of destroying the temple had been provable, then Jesus could have been brought before Roman authority as a social agitator worthy of official attention. However, that way was blocked by a failure to obtain consistent witnesses.

So the failure of the temple charge led into the question about whether Jesus was the Son of God, probably meant messianically, given that the question is about the Christ (Matt. 26:62–66//Mark 14:60–64, like Luke 22:66–71). In an event whose importance cannot be overestimated, the messianic question to Jesus becomes an occasion for him to claim authority over his questioners. Jesus simply predicts that God will vindicate him one day soon in a way that they could see. His claim is that God will exalt him to a place at God's right hand, and one day the Son of Man (i.e., Jesus himself) will come on the clouds, as Dan. 7 describes. So what happens to Jesus is not ultimately in the hands of the Jewish leadership but in the hands of God. The question becomes whether God will stand up for and vindicate this messianic claimant.

At the Jewish examination of Jesus, what he has said either is a rightful claim to be exalted by God or is blasphemy. There was no middle road. This was the ultimate question about Jesus in the debate of the final week. The issue at this examination was whether Jesus was who he claimed to be. The claim in Jesus's reply was that he was the Messiah *and more.* Not only was he the Christ, but he also was the Son of Man, who has the right to sit permanently in God's very presence and exercise final judgment. The Jewish leadership regarded this religious claim about divine exaltation from the earth up as blasphemy. It also allowed them to take a political charge to Pilate that Jesus claimed to lead a kingdom competing with Rome. Jesus was crucified because of the role he claimed to possess. He even supplied the testimony that led to his own conviction. His death was no accident but was purposed even as he chose to enter into the path of suffering and substitution that God had set before him.

The Trial before Pilate

The trial before Pilate rotated around the political issue of a claim for kingship because the Romans did not care that Jesus made more transcendent claims (Matt. 27:11–26//Mark 15:1–15//Luke 23:1–25). This note of Roman skepticism about Jesus's greater claims comes through in the account of John 18:28–38. Initially Pilate appears to desire to let Jesus go, not regarding him as a true threat to Rome or having done anything deserving death. After all, what army did Jesus possess that could threaten this world power? The pressure of the Jewish leadership induces him finally to agree to Jesus's death, despite Pilate's declarations of Jesus's innocence, a point Luke 23 makes several times. Thus Jesus dies unjustly as a result of pressure from the leaders of Judaism, a point Josephus also makes in his report on how Jesus died (*Ant.* 18.63–64). Jesus dies as an innocent.

According to the placard hung on the cross, Jesus dies under the charge of claiming to be "the King of the Jews." For his Jewish opponents, Jesus was killed because he made this claim but even more for the comprehensive authority that he claimed to possess as that figure. They regarded the claim to sit with God as an insult to the unique integrity of God and his honor. In their view, his death would bring an end to this error. For Jesus, the case was in the hands of God.

Resurrection and Divine Vindication from the Earth Up

It is in this context of controversy that the Gospel portraits of the resurrection must be understood. The resurrection is seen as a divine vindication of Jesus's claims that he has the right to sit at God's side. The act is portrayed as God's vote in this dispute. As a vindication of these claims, the resurrection, with its assumed exaltation, means not only that Jesus is alive and that God can give life after death but also that Jesus is who he claimed to be, since God has exalted Jesus into his presence in heaven. In the vindication of Jesus out of death is the affirmation of his uniqueness from the earth up and a divine endorsement of his life and ministry.

The theological development of this understanding of the event is shown in Matt. 28:18. As Jesus declares, God has given him "all authority in heaven and on earth." Divine vindication also appears in how the ministry and church mission are linked in connection to a divine plan revealed in Scripture (Luke 24:44–49). Kingdom hope is affirmed in Peter's claim that the arrival of the Spirit is evidence of God's vindication of Jesus as Lord and Messiah, proving the arrival of the new era (Acts 2:16–39). Divine vindication also surfaces in the teaching that Jesus was resurrected so that there is one ordained to be the judge of the living and the dead (Acts 10:39–42).

All these texts fill in what Jesus claimed during the Jewish examination: one day the leadership would see evidence of God's exaltation of him. For the Gospels, the evidence for Jesus's authority includes the empty tomb, the resurrection, and the place where Jesus ended up as a result of being raised from the dead. Jesus's announcement of exaltation points to who he is. Exaltation means resurrection to God's side, confirming Jesus's divine authority. It is Jesus's authority, both the origin and proof of it, that is the most important topic of the last week of Jesus's ministry.

One of the oldest church creeds we have is the old Roman form of the Apostles' Creed, dating from before the late fourth century.[4] It

4. Philip Schaff, *The Creeds of Christendom*, 6th ed., 3 vols. (1931; reprint, Grand Rapids: Baker, 1977), 1:21–22. The oldest form of the creed that we possess dates to ca. AD 390, but it is referred to by earlier church fathers (see ibid., 1:16–20).

summarizes well what was confessed about Jesus by the early church of that period:

> I believe in God the Father Almighty.
> And in Jesus Christ, his only Son, our Lord; who was born by the Holy Spirit of the Virgin Mary;
> Was crucified under Pontius Pilate and was buried;
> The third day he rose from the dead;
> He ascended into heaven; and sits on the right hand of the Father;
> From there he shall come to judge the quick [living] and the dead.
> And in the Holy Spirit;
> The Holy Church;
> The forgiveness of sins;
> The resurrection of the body.

Here we clearly see the church's understanding that the events of the last week led Jesus to assume a position of unequaled authority at God's side. Jesus shares in the divine prerogative of judgment and salvation. Jesus is more than a teacher, more than a prophet, and more than a Messiah. He is the uniquely authoritative revelator and Son of God. This is the very reason John opens his Gospel by calling Jesus the Word of God, the one who reveals the Father as no other can. The ultimate last word in all of this is what God is said to have done at the end of the final week of Jesus's ministry.

Conclusion

Jesus, the Uniquely Authoritative Revelator of God and Kingdom Hope

The thrust of Jesus's teaching was that he brought the promised new era of the rule of God. As prophet and as the one hoped for, Jesus both explained the divine program and embodied divine presence and authority. His mission began with and focused on Israel, but his ultimate goal was to bring God's presence and promise to the world, opening up understanding of who we are and why we were placed here on earth.

The kingdom presence that Jesus inaugurated opened the way for God's victory and the Spirit of God's coming because the forgiveness that leads to life came through Jesus. Opening up access to the grace of God, Jesus made possible a way of life that honors God. It is a way of life that reflects God's character and will. It forms us into a community and leads us into being God's children.

Jesus's mission started on the premise that the nation and ultimately the world would need this message of hope. He understood that the renunciation of self-focus bound up in his call to turn to God meant that many in the world would not accept the invitation to be a part of God's people. To accept God's gift of grace means to acknowledge one's own need and limitations. Whether expressed as faith or repentance, the kingdom blessing comes only to those who embrace their need for life in the way God has established it.

At the center of this newly announced divine program stood the one who makes its presence and continuance possible. Jesus portrayed himself as the Son of Man, a human being who possessed divine authority seen mostly in a series of acts that pointed to his divine prerogatives. According to Scripture, Jesus is far more than a prophet. He is far more than a king who promised deliverance. Jesus is the revealer and explainer of God's plan, as well as the bridge of access to God. As the unique revelator of God and as the Son of Man, Jesus is what the Synoptics and John portray him to be. Whether that story is told from the earth up or from heaven down, the story of Jesus's uniqueness is the same. For the Synoptics, Jesus emerges as the Messiah-Lord, the one who possesses divine authority clothed in humanity. John's Gospel says it more directly from the very start: Jesus is the Word of God and is God, God in the flesh (John 1:1, 14).

The painting known as *Christ before the High Priest* by Gerrit van Honthorst is my favorite depiction of the Jewish examination scene.[1] It resides at the National Gallery in London and illustrates the purpose of this study. It shows Caiaphas staring at Jesus and seemingly giving his opinion about Jesus, while Jesus looks back at him skeptically. Who was this Jesus, and what was he about? Rather than having the high priest express his view, we have summarized the portrait that comes from Matthew, Mark, Luke, and John.

Beyond the evangelists, two types of people tend to inquire about Jesus. One type searches for who he is. With sometimes skeptical eyes, they ask, "How can we know who Jesus is?" It is a fair question. Throughout this book we have tried to suggest why the central strands of the evangelists' portraits have credibility and can be taken seriously. The themes we have traced run through the array of strands in the Jesus tradition. We contend that these central strands of the Gospel tradition tell us who Jesus was and is. The other type of inquirer, having discovered where Jesus can be found, tries to appreciate the

1. http://www.nationalgallery.org.uk/paintings/gerrit-van-honthorst-christ-before-the-high-priest.

depth of his message even more. The premise of this book is that our glimpse of Jesus is far clearer when he is seen according to the central strands of Scripture rather than viewed in the reconstructions that pick and choose from the four portraits we have of Jesus.

Our study, building on ground detailed by the book *Jesus according to Scripture*, has tried to show how the Gospel writers told the story of Jesus mostly from the earth up (Synoptics), but also from heaven down (John). In the end, the two portraits are not as divergent as they might initially appear—if one keeps the first-century Jewish context in view and maintains an eye on where the diversely expressed portraits land. The church has tended to leave behind an appreciation that people came to realize Jesus's uniqueness in the Gospel accounts at various times and in various ways. The church has often replaced this sense of discovery with an appropriate concern for the result of Christology, a high Christology at that. Yet seeing how Jesus emerged as unique, how he is portrayed from the earth up as well as from heaven down, is a full story the church needs to be able to tell. That comprehensive portrait discloses an ultimate unity between the Jesus of history and the Christ of faith, and between the Synoptics and John. What emerges from these portraits is a singular figure who brings kingdom hope.

Jesus's challenge, which he set out from Scripture and through his sayings and acts, was that God's long-promised and longed-for kingdom rule had broken into creation through his ministry. God's promise of hope and life, the provision of the Spirit, forgiveness, and a vindicated rule had come in him. Jesus from the earth up is a powerful figure, who makes what people think of him and his mission the primary question that one must face in life.

The question of Jesus is primary because it asks of us not only who Jesus is but also who we are as God's creatures. If one seeks to know oneself or find life, one must measure oneself against the Creator and his plan. Jesus never is assessed alone, as if his identity were a historical or academic curiosity or merely a matter of private opinion. For what we think of Jesus reveals what we think of ourselves, our capabilities, and our needs. He puts us in the context of a larger world and before the one Creator God. He keeps us from making ourselves into gods. Who Jesus is and why he came represents a central query about life and its purpose. Jesus is the revelator of God but also the revelator of our hearts before God.

John's Gospel poses the issue this way: "The law was given through Moses; grace and truth came through Jesus Christ. No one has ever seen God; the only Son, who is in the bosom of the Father, he has made him known" (John 1:17–18). Later, John cites Jesus's own words in prayer and adds, "Now this is eternal life: that they know you, the only true God, and Jesus Christ, whom you have sent" (John 17:3 NIV).

This is why understanding that Jesus never claimed to be one more religious great among others is so important. Our world prefers to present Jesus as one among many. That sells him far short. Jesus never allowed such a domesticated option for who he is. Jesus claimed to be unique in his authority as the Son of Man and the unique bearer of the hope of God's rule. As the revelator of God testified to by God from the earth up, Jesus argues that knowing God means being related to Jesus as well. In coming to know Jesus, we will come to understand ourselves, our neighbor, our work, our world, and our Creator. In the process we find everlasting life in kingdom hope that is both now and forever from the earth up.

Author Index

Scripture Index

Mark

Luke

John

Acts

Romans

1 Corinthians

2 Corinthians

Galatians

Ephesians

Subject Index